General editor: Graham Ha[...]

CW00735313

Brodie's Notes on Thomas Hardy's

Tess of the D'Urbervilles

Graham Handley MA PhD
Formerly principal lecturer in English, College of All Saints, Tottenham

Pan Books London, Sydney and Auckland

First published 1986 by Pan Books Ltd,
Cavaye Place, London SW10 9PG
9 8 7 6 5 4 3
© Pan Books Ltd 1986
ISBN 0 330 50235 2
Photoset by Parker Typesetting Service, Leicester
Printed and bound in Great Britain by
Richard Clay Ltd, Bungay, Suffolk

Contents

References in these notes are to the Pan Classics edition of *Tess of the D'Urbervilles* but as each chapter is analysed separately, the Notes may be used with any edition of the book.

Preface

The intention throughout this study aid is to stimulate and guide, to encourage the reader's *involvement* in the text, to develop disciplined critical responses and a sure understanding of the main details in the chosen text.

Brodie's Notes provide a summary of the plot of the play or novel followed by act, scene or chapter summaries, each of which will have an accompanying critical commentary designed to underline the most important literary and factual details. Textual notes will be explanatory or critical (sometimes both), defining what is difficult or obscure on the one hand, or stressing points of character, style or plot on the other. Revision questions will be set on each act or group of chapters to test the student's careful application to the text of the prescribed book.

The second section of each of these study aids will consist of a critical examination of the author's art. This will cover such major elements as characterization, style, structure, setting, theme(s) or any other aspect of the book which the editor considers needs close study. The paramount aim is to send the student back to the text. Each study aid will include a series of general questions which require a detailed knowledge of the set book; the first of these questions will have notes by the editor of what *might* be included in a written answer. A short list of books considered useful as background reading for the student will be provided at the end.

Graham Handley

The author and his work

Thomas Hardy was born on 2 June 1840 in a brick and thatch house at Upper Bockhampton, a hamlet in the parish of Stinsford near Dorchester in Dorset. Hardy chose to spend most of his life near his roots, building himself a house – Max Gate – close by after his major literary successes. Hardy's father was a buoyant and kindly man, a master mason or builder, quite well off for most of his life, but lacking in ambition. He was devoted to his music – Hardys had played and sung the music at Stinsford Parish Church for over a hundred years – and this interest was communicated to and inherited by his son. Hardy's deep love of this traditional music is reflected in his portrait of the Mellstock choir in his early novel, *Under the Greenwood Tree.* As a boy he learned to tune the fiddle, and played it as a young man at weddings and festivals. He would also join in the dancing, sometimes weeping with emotion.

He was greatly influenced by and devoted to his mother. She was an omniverous reader and a woman of strong character – 'the stuff of which great men's mothers are made', as a character in Hardy's powerful novel, *Far From the Madding Crowd*, observes in his fictional world. Hardy was a delicate child, and he did not attend school until he was eight years old. But such was his mental precocity, together with the atmosphere of books and music in his home and the attractions of the countryside around him, that he soon made progress. He had read Dryden's translation of Virgil and Dr Johnson's unusual novel *Rasselas* before he entered Dorchester day school, where he won his first prize at the age of fourteen. He had already made great strides in Latin, and was soon able to read Virgil in the original. He also read Shakespeare, Scott, Milton and some of the popular novelists of his own day. Soon he was learning French and German, but it would be true to say that the Bible was perhaps his main sustained area of study. He knew much of it by heart, and taught in the local Sunday school. He appears to have been a popular boy with his contemporaries, though in some ways he was of a withdrawn temperament, often seeking solitude. He had gained much insight into the social life and nature around him; always the traditions, rituals and superstitions of the villagers and their way of life were present to the developing imagination of the boy. From them he was to create some of his great fiction and, in his eyes, his no less important poetry.

When he was twenty years old Hardy went into the offices of an ecclesiastical architect in Dorchester. Hardy formed the habit of getting up early to study, and added Greek to the Latin he had already acquired. Later Hardy went to London, still working as an architect and restorer, but acquiring a much greater artistic culture from his stay in the capital. He visited art galleries and libraries, and read widely in science and philosophy. He was influenced by Charles Darwin, whose *Origin of the Species* was published in 1859. By the age of thirty Hardy was intellectually an agnostic and, despite his architecturally based career – and here he was certainly competent – he was turning towards writing. He produced some verses and a novel called *The Poor Man and the Lady*, which was rejected by Macmillan. In 1871 he paid a firm to publish his next attempt in fiction, *Desperate Remedies*. It is an uneven and largely melodramatic piece of work, but it has a certain emotional power and the morbid tendency which was to characterize his much later fictional work in particular.

In 1872 *Under the Greenwood Tree* was published. Although this is a Wessex idyll, it has the rustic humour which is typical of Hardy, a loving and warm portrait of the Mellstock choir and of nature, as well as a wayward if sympathetic heroine in Fancy Day. *A Pair of Blue Eyes*, the next novel, shows a major advance in structure, having moments of poignant and lyrical intensity. During this time Hardy had met Emma Gifford on one of his church restoration tours; she was a religious and rather solitary woman, conscious that she was better born than Hardy. But despite this they were married in September 1874 on the strength of Hardy's next novel, *Far From the Madding Crowd*. This appeared in one of the leading magazines of the day, the *Cornhill*, being serialized from January to November 1874 before appearing in volume form. It was his first real success.

It was followed by *The Hand of Ethelberta* (1876), something of a failure, before the great novel, *The Return of Native* (1878), established Hardy as one of the major novelists of the century and indeed of all time. As he wrote on his moods became progressively more sombre and tragic. There were two great novels in the 1880s, *The Major of Casterbridge* (1886) and *The Woodlanders* (1887), both epitomizing the fated man. The first of these has the superb selling-of-the-wife scene at the beginning which carries with it the terrible nemesis for the leading character, Michael Henchard. The second is notable for the loyalty and devotion of Marty South to the ill-fated and self-effacing Giles Winterborne. But it is impossible to do justice in two sentences to the complexity, craftsmanship and sheer imaginative verve of these novels. Set in his beloved Wessex, they are imbued with Hardy's tragic irony, the irony of personal interaction, of irrevocable decision, of human relationships caught in these decisions, and subject to circumstances and coincidences in which the presence of a malign fate is evident.

In 1891 the three-volume edition of *Tess of the D'Urbervilles* was published, and it soon became Hardy's most popular novel, being translated into many languages and bringing, as so often with Hardy, controversy with it. One of the original pre-titles was *Too Late Beloved*, and two of the scenes involving Tess's midnight baptism of her child Sorrow and the location of her seduction (or rape) by Alec D'Urberville were cut from the serial version. This was to conform to the standards of Victorian morality, or rather prudery, but Hardy restored both incidents when the book appeared.

His final novel, *Jude the Obscure* (1895), christened by one critic 'Jude the Obscene', traces the struggles of a working man to gain entry to Christminster (the thinly disguised name for Oxford) and his failure in life and in marriage. Again the intensity of the conception is tragic: Jude dies in poverty and obscurity, a martyr to man's inhumanity to man, particularly if that man is of a different class and background to those accepted as the privileged heirs to the highest education. The reception of this radical novel, with its direct challenging of a code of judgement which is fundamentally immoral, was largely bitter and hostile. Like *Tess*, *Jude* probed conventional conceptions of marital and sexual relationships with an unerring emphasis on truth at the expense of social and religious fallacies. Though he had for some years been settled in his home at Max Gate, and though he was widely recognized as a great writer, Hardy turned his back on the novel after the hostility to *Jude* and devoted his literary energies to poetry, his first and perhaps his deepest love.

At this period of his life there is little doubt that there was growing domestic disharmony between Hardy and his wife Emma. Their marriage had been childless, she was aware of their (supposed) social differences, and even had delusions of her own grandeur which included the belief that she was a superior writer to her husband. She died in 1912, and Hardy was stricken with remorse, his poignant verses and his visits to places he had visited with her all those years before testifying to his personal anguish. Nevertheless, in 1914 he married a woman nearly forty years his junior, Florence Dugdale, and took her home to Max Gate. Throughout their life together he continued to write poems – often about Emma – sensitive, lyrical creations of exquisite concentration, craftsmanship and feeling. The greatest living novelist was hailed as a major poet, and there are certainly critics today who value Hardy's poetry above his prose.

Be that as it may, honours were showered upon him in his lifetime, especially after the publication of *The Dynasts*, a verse-drama of the Napoleonic Wars. He received a number of honorary degrees (ironic this for a man who had never formally progressed beyond grammar school). The Order of Merit was bestowed on him in 1910, the Gold Medal of the Royal Society of Literature in 1911. His greatest pleasure perhaps came from his being granted the Freedom of the Borough of Dorchester. He himself supervised the printing of many of his works in his own lifetime, and left a considerable amount of money when he died. Before then he had virtually written a selective autobiographical account of himself, though it was published as if it was the work of his second wife.

The irony which pervaded so much of his work was given a dramatic twist after his death. It was decided that the man who had never sought fame should be buried in Westminster Abbey. There were quarrels over the precedence for tickets, and the agnostic was interred in England's national shrine. The body was cremated, the ashes placed in Poet's Corner beneath a spadeful of Dorset earth, while his heart was carried back to Stinsford and buried in the grave of his first wife. The final act is ironically consonant with his greatest fiction and his unique spirit.

Writing and publication of
Tess of the D'Urbervilles

It was as early as March 1887 that Hardy was offered a large sum for a book which would be as long as *The Woodlanders*. The offer was made by Tillotson's of Bolton, and the form of publication was to be that of a serial. Hardy contracted to deliver the first few instalments of the novel before the end of June 1889. But Hardy and his wife spent the spring and part of the summer of that year socializing in London, and the first part of the manuscript of the novel was not sent to the Tillotsons until September. In August Hardy had fixed upon the title as being 'Too late, Beloved!', but there were of course problems to be encountered in this late Victorian period in having a publisher of popular serial fiction take easily to a seduction and the unclerical baptism of an illegitimate child. At proof stage of the first half of the novel, the publishers apparently realized the full extent of Hardy's treatment and the nature of the work they were about to issue and requested the deletion of certain material. Hardy refused to comply, the agreement was cancelled and the firm paid Hardy an agreed sum.

In earlier instances Hardy had agreed to alter details in his work, but here he was obviously very involved with his conception and with the nature of his heroine. He was now in a position to offer his still unfinished novel to the *Graphic* magazine, which had published a story by him some years previously. The *Graphic* paid him £550 for the serial rights, and the novel was also published in the *Nottinghamshire Guardian*. Hardy himself negotiated his own agreement with Harper's in the United States. He continued writing throughout 1890, the second part of the manuscript having been despatched in May. Certain incidents were cut from the serial version. The most important of these were the seduction and the events which precede it, and the midnight baptism of Sorrow. The incident involving Angel carrying the milkmaids across the flood was also deleted, though he did use a wheelbarrow to transport them. These cuts were restored when the book edition was issued in December 1891. Its serial run in the *Graphic* lasted from July to December of that year.

But Hardy was essentially loyal to his original conception, and in May 1891 'The Midnight Baptism' was published in the *Fortnightly Review*. On 14 November 1891 the *National Observer* published 'Saturday Night in Arcady', Hardy's adaptation of another chapter in *Tess*, the Chaseborough incident and the ensuing seduction. After the novel was issued in three volumes in December it sold very quickly, and this despite the strictures of reviewers like the one in *The Saturday Review*, who wrote that 'Mr Hardy, it must be conceded, tells an unpleasant story in a very unpleasant way.'

Plot and background

Plot

The main plot of the novel is quite straightforward. John Durbey-field, who earns his living by buying and selling in a small rural way, learns from an antiquarian parson that he is descended from the once rich and aristocratic D'Urberville family. He immediately gets an inflated idea of his own importance, turns to drink, and is not well enough to take the beehives to the Casterbridge Market the next day. His eldest daughter Tess and her young brother Abraham set off to do so, but Tess dozes off and the Durbeyfield horse pulling the cart is killed when they collide with a mailcoach.

Tess blames herself for the increased poverty of her family and, pressed by her mother, visits her supposed 'relations' the D'Urbervilles, in the hope that they might give her a job. On the insistence of Alec D'Urberville, who is fascinated by Tess's beauty, Mrs D'Urberville employs Tess. The latter goes there in all innocence, but she is subjected to much pestering by Alec. On a trip with her fellow workers to a neighbouring town Tess finds herself alone on the return journey; she is overtaken by Alec, who seduces her.

Some four months after her arrival at the D'Urberville home at Trantridge, Tess goes back to her parents. Her mother taxes her with not having got Alec to marry her. In the following year she gives birth to a sickly child, gets a job with the harvesters and then, realizing that her child is dying, baptizes it at home with her brothers and sisters for congregation. She remains at home throughout the winter and then, two or three years after she has returned from her 'relations' at Trantridge she takes a job as a dairymaid in the distant Valley of the Great Dairies at Talboth-ays. There she works for Dairyman Crick, lives with three other girls, Marian, Izz and Retty, and meets a student farmer, Angel Clare, who had seen Tess some years before.

Tess and Angel are attracted to each other (the three girls mentioned above are all in love with Angel). Angel is the son of a clergyman and, after some time, he pays court to Tess. She at first reacts strongly against this in view of her guilty past, and tries unsuccessfully on a number of occasions to tell him of her affair with Alec D'Urberville. Clare meanwhile returns home, preparing his parents for his coming marriage to Tess, though he does not give too many details about her. His father ironically reveals that he has been insulted by Alec D'Urberville when he has taxed him and his sinful ways.

Clare returns to Talbothays and proposes to Tess. She refuses him, but eventually succumbs despite her fears. She writes to tell her mother, and breaks the news to the other girls. On her wedding night she finally confesses her past transgression to Clare. He is horrified and will not forgive her. He determines to go to Brazil to explore the possibilities of sheep-farming. In an impulsive moment, and having learned that Izz Huett loves him, Clare asks her to accompany him. She accepts, but tells Clare that no one could ever love him as much as Tess did. To her discomfort, Clare now tells her to forget his offer.

Tess uses the money that Clare had left her to relieve her parents' sufferings, but although hard-pressed herself, cannot bring herself to apply to his parents for aid. Clare, meanwhile, has been taken ill in Brazil. Tess goes to Flintcomb Ash to work – Marian is there too – 'a starve-acre place', where she learns from Marian of Clare's invitation to Izz. She eventually makes an abortive journey to see Clare's parents, but they are out and she is humiliated. Later she re-meets Alec, who has been converted by the example of Mr Clare into a Free-Church preacher. He soon loses his religious fervour in his born-again passion for Tess. The latter writes pathetically to her husband, returns home though much pressed by Alec D'Urberville. Her father dies and with him the tenure of the cottage. The family are forced to move, Alec steps in to make Tess his mistress, and Izz and Marian write to Angel to 'Look to your wife.'

When Angel, worn in health, arrives home he reads Tess's last letter in which she says that 'It is all injustice that I have received at your hands.' He sets off in search of Tess, learns from her mother that she is at Sandbourne, and makes his way there, where he finds her living with Alec. After Angel has left Tess kills Alec, and she and Angel spend an idyllic week in the New Forest before she is arrested. She virtually bequeathes her sister Liza-Lu to Clare, and is hanged for the murder of Alec, the novel ending with the much-quoted ' "Justice" was done, and the President of the Immortals, in Aeschylean phrase, had ended his sport with Tess.'

Background

Hardy was brought up with the Dorset countryside as his background, and after a few years in London he returned to these roots. They form the ever-present locale for the actions of his characters, giving to his novels a sense of time and place, a historical truth. The reader of *Tess of the D'Urbervilles* will be immediately aware of Hardy's love for that countryside, for his pictures of it are vivid and clear. His home town of Dorchester is the Casterbridge of Wessex, and in *Tess* the three main characters go as far as Sandbourne, Hardy's coinage for Bournemouth. Hardy took great care with interior and exterior description: the buildings are faithful likenesses, even to the dreadful portraits on the stairs at the Wellbridge Manor House, while he visited Stonehenge and other places in the novel to get the topography absolutely right. This is revealed in his *Life*, supposedly written by his widow, but almost certainly by Hardy himself where, we are told, he 'explored in greater detail than ever before the scenes of the story'.

Apart from particular identifications, Nature itself plays a major part in the novel, with the lushness of Talbothays forming a pointed contrast to the bleakness of Flintcomb-Ash, and the seduction in the Chase may be compared with the violation of the birds which Tess is forced to kill in the wood. The natural background has a very strong seasonal flavour, the oppressive heat at Talbothays conveying the atmosphere conducive to the love and courtship of Tess by Angel. Note that it is winter when they marry and separate, and autumn into winter when Tess goes from Marlott and settles in the cold of Flintcomb-Ash. The changes in nature are the permanent background to the changes in the circumstances of the main characters in the novel.

The natural background, as one might expect, is closely connected with the agricultural labours and labourers. The range of Hardy's countrymen embraces the indigent poor like John Durbeyfield and his family, where haggling is a way of life, to Farmer Groby, whose work force are on piece-rates, to

Dairyman Crick, who provides accommodation for his milkmaids who enjoy a reasonable standard of living while they have jobs. While Hardy believes that there is something noble about man's association with the soil, and that a rustic community possessed a self-sufficiency unknown to urban life, he is also a great critic of living conditions. The village may be a family unit, where people's affairs are common knowledge, but Hardy knew that agriculture was decaying. There is internal evidence (from the references to Brazil) that *Tess* is set in the late 1860s, early 1870s and, as G. M. Trevelyan, the social historian, wrote, 'The greatest single event of the 'seventies, fraught with immeasurable consequences for the future, was the collapse of agriculture.'

That Hardy was aware of this there is no doubt. Hardy records (Chapter 51) that 'A depopulation was going on', and country market towns like Chaseborough (Cranborne) were decaying. But although old customs were dying out, we notice that at Marlott the woman's club-walking remained. Antiquated deeds of leasehold property made life more uncertain as, for instance, with John Durbeyfield, who held the tenure only during his lifetime. From the rustics' conversations, which form a kind of ballad chorus to the main strands of the novel, there is a wealth of information to be gathered about the daily attitudes and feelings of the working community, their superstitions, their extreme fatalism, their 'fetichistic' religion (Chapter 16) and their acceptance of life as it comes in a small village community. Dairyman Crick is in some ways typical. On Sundays he is a prominent figure 'in shining broadcloth in his family pew at church', outwardly conformist, but he has a superstitious side to his nature, as we see when he thinks of witchcraft when the milk is short, or determines to go to a conjuror when the butter will not come. He is full of omens and rustic anecdotes (we note how he interprets the cock's crow when Angel and Tess leave on their honeymoon), and in fact the scenes at Talbothays show how steeped Hardy is in country lore and practice. 'Every village', he says in Chapter 10, 'has its idiosyncrasy, its constitution, often its own code of morality.' We might note the Marlott reaction to Tess's sin, which after some criticism, later to be remembered, gives way to a considerate acceptance on the part of her fellow-labourers as she feeds her baby.

The critical commentary makes clear that journeys in the novel are an important part of the action. In those days the ordinary men or women walked for the most part. When the novel opens, John Durbeyfield is walking from Shaston (Shaftesbury) to Marlott (Marnhull), a distance of about eight miles. When Tess goes to Emminster (Beaminster) to call on the Clares, she walks fifteen miles each way. Obviously the rich had carriages or could hire them, but for the villagers the boundary of their village was often the extent of their knowledge of the world. But *Tess* registers the onset of change in many ways. The railway had come within an hour's ride of Beaminster and, as we remember from a crucial scene in the novel, the milk from Talbothays is sent to London by rail (Chapter 30). Even more important is the hiring of the steam threshing machine, when 'The old men on the rising straw-rick talked of the past days when they had been accustomed to thresh with flails on the oaken barn-floor; when everything, even winnowing, was effected by hand-labour, which to their thinking, though slow, produced better results.' Hardy manages to convey the rule of the monster here, with the workers as slaves to the new era of mechanized power.

Hardy was concerned about working conditions, perhaps not in the sense of active reform, but certainly in the Dickensian sense of revealing what they were. A farm labourer worked for as long as his master wanted him to work. We remember Tess's afternoon in the shed reed-drawing (Chapter 43), or the farmer ordering that the rick should be finished 'that night, since there was a moon by which they could see to work' (Chapter 48). It would be rash to refuse, since labour was cheap and easily come by. At that 'starve-acre' place Flintcomb-Ash, the cheapness of female labour and the piece-work payments are sufficient indication of the lowering economic circumstances.

Hardy also gives some indication of the caste or class-system prevailing at the time. Angel is a trainee in effect under Mr Crick for a period of six months, but his division from the ordinary work force is seen in his eating his food separately in the chimney-corner. Although he does the same work as the others, he is called variously 'Mr Clare' or 'Sir'. When Parson Tringham is telling John Durbeyfield about his ancestors he calls him 'Durbeyfield', while the haggler calls him 'Sir'. Alec D'Urberville from his faked eminence merely refers to the Trant-ridge people as 'work-folk', and we always feel a certain conde-scension in his attitude to Tess, who is certainly of that class.

There was widespread poverty in the agricultural villages, since wages were low, and were often seasonal only (as at harvest time). Public houses were open all day, and there were many, like Marian and John Durbeyfield, who found consolation in drink. Hardy finds a neat turn of irony in this when he observes that 'smock-frocked arithmeticians, leaning on their ploughs or hoes, would enter into calculations of great nicety to prove that parish relief was a fuller provision for a man in his old age than any which could result from savings out of their wages during a whole lifetime.' The picture as so often with Hardy has its pathos, the excuse being the need for the only daily relief that they know.

We have noticed the range of Hardy's background with its provision of authenticity – note the efficiency of the postal services. Note also the time it takes the police to catch up with Tess, though perhaps an unlikely length of time, an indication certainly of the importance of the background to Hardy, who obviously felt that Stonehenge must be invested with a symbol-ism appropriate to its original sacrificial functions. Then there are the village amusements traditionally connected with country festivals, such as the May-time 'club-walking' and following dance at Marlott. We note also the Saturday trip to Chase-borough, typical of the visits to fairs on market days, and we remember the dancing which delays Tess and thus inadvertently leads to her seduction. One of the moving aspects of the immediate background is seen at Talbothays, where all the cows have their individual names and the milkers adapt themselves to their individual peculiarities.

Chapter summaries, critical commentaries, textual notes and revision questions

Phase the First Chapter 1

Jack Durbeyfield, the haggler, is walking home (somewhat unsteadily) when he meets Parson Tringham the antiquary. The parson tells him that he is descended from the 'ancient and knightly' family of the D'Urbervilles, now 'extinct – as a county family'. When the parson has gone Durbeyfield rests, summons a passing boy to him, tells him of his noble antecedents and orders the boy to get a carriage for him.

Commentary

Hardy's ironic conception is evident in this first chapter. Parson Tringham sets Durbeyfield on the road to self-importance which is going to affect other members of his family, nost notably Tess. One of the themes of the novel is sounded immediately, that of the influence of the past on the present, the 'fallen' family of the D'Urbervilles anticipating the 'fallen' nature of man, and woman, and having particular application to Tess. Notice the natural ease of the dialogue, the pedantic display of knowledge from the parson, the self-congratulatory response of 'Sir John', and the fact that Tess, who is to be the central figure in the action of the novel, is only mentioned in passing as taking part in the 'women's club-walking'.

Shaston The old name of Shaftesbury, which Hardy uses.
haggler i.e. buying and selling whatever he could pick up.
D'Urbervilles Slightly adapted by Hardy from the Turbervilles of Bere Regis, the original of Kingsbere in the novel.
William the Conqueror He defeated King Harold at the Battle of Hastings (1066) and ruled England until his death in 1087.
Battle Abbey Roll Battle Abbey was built by William the Conqueror on the site of the Battle of Hastings, its roll being a list of those who accompanied the Conqueror to England.
Pipe Rolls These related to all matters, financial affairs connected with the Crown.
King Stephen Reigned 1135–54; King John 1199–1216; Edward II 1307–27; Oliver Cromwell (Lord Protector from 1653) 1649–58; Charles II 1660–85.

Knights Hospitallers These were the Knights of St John, one of the independent religious orders of knighthood founded during the Crusades with responsibility for tending the sick.

Knights of the Royal Oak An order invented by Hardy, drawing no doubt on the escape of Charles II (then Prince Charles) by hiding in an oak tree after the battle of Worcester (1651).

wold Old (in the local accent or dialect).

raise our smoke i.e. live.

Purbeck-marble Limestone used for slender shafts in the interiors of Gothic churches, from the 'isle' of Purbeck (Dorset), a peninsula connected to the mainland by an isthmus.

"how are the mighty fallen" See 2 Samuel, 1, 19 and Chapter 54 (p.405), where the line is inscribed on John Durbeyfield's tombstone – an indication of Hardy's structural awareness.

The Pure Drop Now The Crown, which has The Pure Drop Bar.

lath-like Very thin.

this present afternoon, p.m. Note the humour – 'Sir John' repeats himself in his tipsy state.

'twaddn' It wasn't.

gr't Great.

skillentons Skeletons.

noggin Small mug holding a quarter of a pint.

black-pot Black pudding – pig's blood and meat.

chitterlings Intestines of the pig, fried and stuffed.

da'ter Daughter – the first, seemingly casual, reference to Tess.

vamp Tramp, another dialect usage.

Chapter 2

The village of Marlott is described, together with its surroundings and historical interest and the tradition of 'club-walking'. The walkers come round by the Pure Drop Inn, and notice John Durbeyfield being driven home in his tipsy state. Tess is embarrassed by this, and forbids any joking about it; the walk ends in a field for dancing, and three young students on a walking tour appear at the gate. The youngest of the brothers stays for a while, dances with one of the girls (not Tess), and goes on, later looking back from the rise of the next hill, seeing Tess below looking after him. He notes her appeal, but walks on.

Commentary

Note the perspective of the natural description which conveys a sense of permanence and tradition. The legend about the killing of the white hart has a significant forward-looking effect when we consider what is to happen to Tess – an unobtrusive structural awareness again on Hardy's part. The innocence and the local tradition of the 'club-walking' are stressed, ritual being an important part of country life, and this set-piece forms a humorous contrast with the arrival of 'Sir John'. We observe at once Tess's physical attraction and her pride – and of course her capacity to suffer, here on her father's account. But she is resilient, and the 'Phases of her childhood' are a considered appraisal of her innocence. Her wearing a red ribbon – red is to be associated with her throughout, through strawberries, roses, her lips and blood – is a mark of her physical distinction. Again there is a certain oblique cunning about the way the three young men are introduced; since we know later who they are, the implication is that Fate has a hand in things, for Angel does not meet Tess on this occasion. Hardy is adept, as we see from this, at what-might-have-been, a truth to life which gives his fiction the intensity of realism.

plashed Bent down.
Cerealia Ceres, the Roman goddess of corn and agriculture, had festivals held in her honour.
votive Performed or dedicated.
Old Style days i.e. before the change of the calendar in 1752, when it was put forward to bring it into line with the other European countries.
a peeled willow wand Thought to make for fertility, a reminiscence of the Roman festival of Lupercalia.
'I have no pleasure in them' See Ecclesiastes, 12,1.
Lord-a-Lord i.e. exclamation, like 'Good God'.
chaise Light, open horse-drawn carriage.
factotum i.e. someone employed to do all kinds of work.
'Bless thy simplicity, Tess' Another stress-mark of Tess's innocence.
market-nitch i.e. drink consumed at the market or on market-day.
twelfth ... ninth ... fifth All indicative of the innocence and unworldliness mentioned above.
uncribbed, uncabined An echo of Shakespeare's *Macbeth*, Act III, Scene 4, line 24, – 'I am cabin'd, cribb'd, confin'd' – i.e. locked in.
hoydens Young irresponsible girls.
A Counterblast to Agnosticism Hardy is intent on authenticating his period, a time of faith *and* expressions of doubt, hence his choice of this as a likely title for a book.
clipsing and colling Hugging and kissing.
her life's battle ... Compare this simple image with the echo of it which is found when Tess's child Sorrow dies.

Norman blood ... Victorian lucre Note the cynicism – and irony – of this comment on the fact that money can buy anything.

She was so modest ... This is how Angel sees Tess until her later revelation – and it is what she truly is despite her 'sin' with Alec.

Chapter 3

Tess ponders on the experience but, worried by her father's state, soon makes her way home. She finds her mother surrounded by the other children, still doing the washing which was begun at the beginning of the week. Mrs Durbeyfield tells Tess of the discovery of their noble status, says that 'Sir John' has gone to the ale-house, and soon follows, nominally to fetch him home. After sending Abraham to get them, Tess finally has to go herself.

Commentary

Tess's susceptibility is apparent in her reaction to the impression Angel Clare has made upon her. The description of Joan Durbeyfield reveals a feckless woman, and the interior of the home is drawn by Hardy with unsparing realism. There is an effective contrast between mother and daughter; the mother is bowed down by domestic poverty, her only escape from it being the news (of their supposedly new status), her husband's illness, her need to sit with him and drink to forget the household trap. Tess is strongly moral and responsible by contrast, deploring her father's need to 'get up his strength' by going to Rolliver's. The gap between mother and daughter is stressed, and perhaps it is epitomized by Mrs Durbeyfield's reliance on the *Compleat Fortune-Teller*, a book which carries its own irony in the context of the novel. The dependence of the children, Tess's assumption of responsibility, are important pointers towards the future.

treading a measure i.e. dancing.

'the soft torments ...' Note that the quotation is given ironically, stressing the mingling of happiness and pain which forecasts Tess's experiences with Angel Clare.

gallopade Lively two-beat rhythm.

'I saw her lie down ...' The song's words in these lines are suggestive of seduction, again an unconscious look forward to Tess's fate.

diment Diamond.

Cubit's Mrs Durbeyfield's pronunciation of 'Cupid', the Roman God of Love.

one-candled spectacle Note the paradox emblematic of poverty.
like a weaver's shuttle Typical of Hardy's acute observation.
wring up i.e. mangle the clothes.
fess Proud.
National School Schools conducted by Voluntary Bodies, here the
  National Society for Promoting the Education of the Poor in the
  Principles of the Established Church, were responsible for much of
  English education before the establishment of the state system in 1870.
mommet ridiculous figure.
think That.
larry Disturbance.
Oliver Grumble's time. . . Saint Charles Mrs Durbeyfield means
  Oliver Cromwell and King Charles.
plim Fill out.
vlee Hired one-horse hackney carriage.
mampus Crowd.
shadder Shadow.
rafted Put out, disturbed.
concretions i.e. facts (from which she could not escape).
Revised Code This publication (1862) attempted to relate the size of
  each grant to a school to its pupils' achievements.
Hope and Modesty These abstract names ironically embody qualities
  possessed by Tess.
the Durbeyfield ship . . . to sail . . . under hatches The sustained image
  is a wry comment on the family dependence on the breadwinner.
the poet whose philosophy. . . 'Nature's holy plan' The reference is to
  Wordsworth (1770–1850), the quotation being from his 'Lines Written
  in Early Spring'.
The village was shutting its eyes Note the casual but effective
  personification.
bain't Are not.
gone wi' Happened to.
limed . . . caught . . . ensnaring i.e. trapped with bird-lime, a metaphor
  which at once indicates Hardy's love of nature and his concern for
  man.
one-handed clocks i.e. when nobody cared about the time – the
  nearest hour was good enough.

Chapter 4

Tess finds her father and mother drinking in the alehouse;
when she arrives they are talking of her, and of Joan's plan for
her (Tess) to approach their rich 'relatives'. Tess gets them
home, but her father is unable to get up in the small hours, and
Tess and Abraham set out to deliver the beehives. Tess learns
from Abraham of her mother's plans on her behalf with her 'kin'
at Trantridge. Tess and Abraham doze off, but she awakes when

the cart collides with a mail-cart and their horse is killed. The beehives are taken on by a farmer's man, and Tess goes home reproaching herself for bringing ruin on her family.

Commentary

A very significant chapter, conveying the idea that earth is indeed a 'blighted' world for Tess and the Durbeyfields. The description of Rolliver's with the landlady's exaggerated fear of 'officialdom' is rich with humour. There is the irony of the customers seeking 'beatitude', the pleasure of discomfort in the crowded bedroom, the landlady's reiterative cover up, all this makes for comedy, but it is inlaid with pathos – for this is an outlet, an escape, from a life of deprivation. Joan shows her opportunism, influenced of course by what she has found by way of corroboration in the *Fortune-Teller*, and her knowledge that Tess is 'tractable at bottom'. Tess's sense of responsibility – allied to a sense of shame – is seen when she undertakes the journey. There is a build up of tension and pathos as the horse is got ready, and the dialogue between Tess and Abraham symbolizes the concept of Fate, albeit rustically put by Tess, an inherent belief that sufferers are born to experience more suffering. There is a marvellous sense of the dozing dream before the dramatic reality. Note once more the colour effects – the 'crimson drops' of the blood and Tess's pallor – the first relating to killing (Tess thinks of it as murder and it anticipates her later killing of Alec), while the whiteness is her purity. Durbeyfield's senseless pride in the burial of the horse is seen in contradistinction to Tess's unvoiced feeling that 'she regarded herself in the light of a murderess'.

Polynesia The Pacific Islands which look like small spots on a map.
beatitude Supreme blessedness (but generally with religious associations, which makes the remark here ironic).
wide house See Proverbs 21,9.
'cwoffer Chest.
the magnificent pillars of Solomon's temple See 1 Kings 7,15–22,2 and Chronicles 3, 15–17.
Catechism Hardy's irony, for the Catechism is a set of questions and answers on Christianity.
Lard Lord.
gaffer Official.

projick Idea, project.

hanging by it i.e. to be obtained from it.

kin to a coach i.e. related to rich people, but the 'coach' reference, which is followed up by Abraham, has ironic reverberations in the text when we think of the legend of the D'Urberville coach and Tess's coming tragedy.

King Norman's day i.e. the time of William the Conqueror (1066–87).

ride in her coach and wear black clothes See 'kin to a coach' above, and note the 'black clothes' ironically symbolic of death.

sumple Supple.

a fine figure o' fun A bonny, attractive girl.

zeed Saw.

vamping Tramping.

don't get green malt in floor i.e. to become pregnant, according to Hardy himself to 'have a daughter in childbed before she is married'. The phrase, which has passed out of use, has obvious associations with Tess later.

eastings Facing the altar in church.

'count i.e. account, substance.

nater Nature.

Casterbridge Dorchester, where there is still a Saturday market.

kip Keep.

twain Two (of them).

spy-glass Telescope.

stubbard-tree Small apple-tree.

'A blighted one' This is central to the novel – the idea of Fate, and a malign fate at that.

She made him a sort of nest Tess does this in innocence and protection – ironically Alec is to make her one conducive to seduction.

the sigh of some immense sad soul Note the deliberate identification of nature with humanity in this poetic personification.

crimson drops Symbolic of Tess shedding blood – she is later to be a murderess, though after this accident she thinks of herself as one anyway.

the lane showed all its white features . . . Once again an identification of Tess with her surroundings.

chargers The horses of medieval knights.

Her face was dry and pale . . . murderess A very significant anticipation, deliberately placed at the end of the chapter for emphasis, of what Tess is actually to become.

Chapter 5

Tess is persuaded by her mother to pay a visit to her rich 'kin' at Trantridge, though she is reluctant to go and only does so because of her guilt over the death of the horse. Her role in the family is described, with an account of her arrival at The Slopes,

Mrs D'Urberville's home. There follows some background on the family before we return to Tess and her meeting with Alec D'Urberville, the son. The latter appears to be a stereotype of the lady-killer, but he promises to do what he can for Tess, gives her a meal and loads her with roses and strawberries before she goes.

Commentary

Joan is finely manipulative, both of her husband and more particularly of her sensitive daughter. The irony lies in the fact that Tess in her innocence does not fully comprehend what her mother has in mind for her. Her narrow horizons are stressed, and there is every indication of her vulnerability as she ventures into the unknown. There is something poignant about the account of her friendship with the other two girls and of her being a little mother to her own family. The contrast of The Slopes both with what she has known and what she expected is effective and underlines her inexperience, but the real irony of the chapter lies in the account of the Stoke-D'Urbervilles, a spurious line. Thus Tess has come to visit people who are not her relations, and this makes her subsequent fate all the more tragic. Alec appears at first somewhat stagey, but the episode with the strawberry and the forcing of Tess is symbolic of the seduction to come. She is impetuous in her confession of guilt over the dead horse, there is much 'red' imagery symbolic of the blood to be spilt – in seduction and murder – and the author's use of his own voice in commentary on the unfairness of fate, which rarely produces the right lover for the loved one.

slack-twisted i.e. an irregular worker.
memorable morning This is a subtle identification with Tess – the departure is memorable for her.
Malthusian Thomas Malthus (1766–1834), in his *On Population* put forward the theory that population increases faster than the means of subsistence, the results being poverty and suffering.
waiters on Providence i.e. waiting to see what Fate has in store.
The Slopes Note the deliberate choice of name – for it is here that Tess begins to go down the 'slope' despite herself because of Alec's attentions and persistence which ultimately leads to her seduction.
Druidical mistletoe The Druids regarded the mistletoe as sacred, symbolic of fertility – note Angel's placing the mistletoe bough in the bed later, an action imbued with pathos in view of the non-consummation of the marriage.

pollarded i.e. with the tops cut off.

Chapels-of-Ease These are chapels for outlying parishioners, an ironic comparison in view of the irreligious attitude of Alec D'Urberville at this stage – and of his later (temporary) conversion.

framing his intermarriages . . . The implication is of course that the family tree, like the family, is spurious, forged.

hieroglyphic i.e. in symbolic form.

swarthy Alexander Alexander the Great (366–323 BC), the conqueror. This Alexander (Alec is short for the name) is also intent on conquest, hence the irony of the reference.

ramping Rampant (with the suggestion of lustful).

Coz Abbreviation for 'cousin', said ironically by D'Urberville.

he parted her lips and took it in An anticipation of Alec's later seduction of Tess.

blood-red ray Note the image, with its suggestion of passion *and* the shedding of blood.

In the ill-judged execution . . . This omniscient commentary smacks of pessimism, with the idea of the 'missing counterpart' being Angel Clare, who comes 'too late' for his 'beloved' (remember one of the original titles of the novel).

crumby Luscious, fully-formed (appearing to be a woman is the major part of Tess's tragedy).

Chapter 6

Tess stays overnight with a family friend, and goes home the next day. Arrived, she finds that a letter is already there offering her a post in charge of Mrs D'Urberville's poultry-farm. She tries for work in the neighbourhood, but a week later when she arrives back at home she finds that the 'gentleman' has called. Despite her reluctance she decides to go, and takes some comfort that she will be working to get her father another horse.

Commentry

The effect of the roses and strawberries is to enhance Tess's luscious appearance even more, though the prick from the thorn is another ominous anticipation of her being ravished by Alec – an omen which Tess herself recognizes, though not in the Alec context. She is suspicious about the letter (the next letter is 'rather masculine' in its handwriting), and there is a moment of pure pathos when Tess says that she would rather stay at home, and also that she doesn't know why she is fearful. The opportunism of Joan with regard to Alec is evident, the complacency of

Sir John equally so, allied here to his habitual indolence. There is a finely economic moment when Tess walks 'among the gooseberry bushes in the garden, and over Prince's grave'. The term 'gooseberry bush' is a common one for the conception of an illegitimate child, while the horse is the major part of Tess's guilt. Notice that there is a kind of family blackmail to get Tess to go, and that she is incapable of resisting these appeals.

zid Saw.
coll See note on 'clipsing and colling' p.21.
put his hand up to his mistarshers Although the pronunciation of moustaches carries some humour, it is this kind of gesture which makes Alec appear to be the melodramatic rather than the flesh and blood villain.
struck wi' her In contemporary language, 'fancies her'.
dolorifuge Banishing grief (but rather a pedantic word).
golden money to buy fairlings i.e. gold coins (before the days of notes) to buy presents at the fair.

Chapter 7

Tess awakes early and is later dressed suitably by her mother, the latter exultant at the idea of Tess making a conquest. Joan and the children accompany Tess to where she is being met by the spring-cart, Sir John having indicated his willingness to sell his title to Alec. Her family watches as she goes to the waiting cart, but a gig drives up and the driver urges Tess to get in. After a few moments of seeming indecision, she does so all at once. Realizing that Tess has gone, the children begin to cry and even Joan has some misgivings, though she feels that Tess's 'trump card' is her face.

Commentary

Tess's spirit is in abeyance, and as she says 'Do what you like with me, mother', Joan typically proceeds to do just that. She is also cunning in counselling her husband to be careful what he says, for she has a shrewd knowledge of the purity of her daughter's character. We notice how moved Tess is by the parting – in a sense, a farewell to innocence and security, though she does not know it. Her father's offering to sell his title partakes of the grotesque and the pathetic. The drama, or perhaps melodrama, of Alec's sudden appearance is cleverly offset by Tess's guilty obsession, which makes her accept his invitation. The family reaction is moving, but there is a terrible irony in Joan's hope that Tess will succeed if 'she plays her trump card aright', since poor Tess is unconscious of that trump card.

dand Dandy.
zay ... zet Say ... set
Lady Durbeyfield Note the deliberate irony of applying the title when the conversation has taken this commercial turn.
lammicken Clumsy.
horsey young buck Again, the term has the effect of making Alec something of a stereotype or melodramatic character.
choice over her i.e. keen enough to marry her.

Chapter 8

Alec drives recklessly, unnerving Tess, and tricks her into holding him round the waist, later capturing a kiss from her on the promise that he will stop his furious driving. She counters by getting down from the gig, preferring to walk or to get on the cart behind. Alec loses his temper with her, passes off the incident with a laugh, but Tess is unmoved and continues to walk. She ponders on whether to return home, but considers that it would be weak to give up the rehabilitation in such a way.

Commentary

Tess has lost courage somewhat over driving since the death of Prince, but she compensates later by a display of determination. Alec's treatment of the mare – he has in effect broken her in part – foreshadows his treatment of Tess, but the interesting thing is that the mare has killed once, yet another anticipation, since Tess is to kill Alec. He himself says of the mare, 'just after I bought her she nearly killed me'. The control of dialogue exactly captures the temperature of the exchanges and the movement. The 'kiss of mastery' symbolizes the coming seduction, and Tess's attempts to obliterate the spot anticipate her later attempts to rid herself of her sin by confession. In fact, in trying to escape D'Urberville's attentions Tess attempts to escape the effects of them in relation to Angel. Even Alec's bid to hem her in looks forward to the final hemming in – the seduction.

green ... gray The colours symbolize the move from innocence to experience.

humming like a top ... like a splitting stick Hardy has a happy knack of enhancing his narrative by deft, unobtrusive but effective images.
holmberry Holly-berry.
like those of a wild animal Tess is often compared to an animal, as in the sequence at Stonehenge, with the stress on natural instinct and innocence, and even survival.
'I'll break both our necks' An image unconsciously forecasting death, since Alec is to be killed by Tess and she is to be hanged.
the red and ivory of her mouth The colours again of attraction/passion and innocence.

Chapter 9

An account of Tess's place of employment. She learns that Mrs D'Urberville is blind, and that she has to look after this 'community of fowls'. Mrs D'Urberville instructs her in the various things she must do, including whistling, and Alec later reinforces this, since he obviously wishes to be in her company as much as possible. Once she finds him watching her from behind the curtains of his mother's bedstead, but he doesn't interfere with her at this stage.

Commentary

The first part of the chapter is given over to the nature of Mrs D'Urberville's obsession, but the stress on her blindness is important – it means that she cultivates her other senses of hearing and touch. She is an eccentric but vividly drawn. The quality of Tess's imagination is also shown, for she feels of her new charges that she is reminded 'of a Confirmation, in which Mrs D'Urberville was the bishop, the fowls the young people presented, and herself and the maid-servant the parson and curate of the parish bringing them up.' It shows the inward spiritual nature of Tess, a nature more fully revealed later when she has to officiate at the baptism of her own child. That Mrs D'Urberville knows nothing of the 'so-called kinship' is ironic. Tess is somewhat chastened by her efforts to produce the requisite whistles and sounds, but she is conscientious and perseveres. D'Urberville in fact tries to stir Tess up against her tasks, but without success. His use of quotation and song is calculated to influence her, but she is too unsophisticated to notice or even understand. The description of 'a pair of boots ... below the fringe of the curtains' is somewhat humorous, but it shows Alec's persistence in its turn. We feel the narrative tension of his pursuit of Tess though at this time he is prepared to play his cards carefully.

copyholders Holders of land whose tenure depended on copies of a manorial court roll (instead of 'deeds'). It was sometimes renewable on payment of a fee.

Strut ... Phena Significant names, the first reminiscent of the bravado and conceit of Alec, the second perhaps an echo of the name of one of Hardy's cousins with whom he was reputedly in love at one stage – Tryphena.

draggled Wet and dirty.

the old lady had never heard a word ... This contributes to the irony of the situation, and is reflective of Alec's cunning.

like _Im_-patience on a monument An echo of 'Like Patience on a monument', from Shakespeare's _Twelfth Night_ (II, 4, 116). The altered quotation shows Alec's passion.

bullies i.e. bullfinches.

'Take, O take those lips away'. The first line of a song which opens Act IV, Scene 1, of Shakespeare's _Measure for Measure_. The relevance here is apparent – Tess's lips are temptation.

sculptural severity Notice how even a casual phrase like this shows Hardy's awareness – it echoes the '_Im_-patience on a monument', with Tess firm in her purpose of resistance.

out of her books i.e. out of favour.

Chapter 10

It was the custom of the Trantridge work-people to go to Chaseborough – 'a decayed market-town two or three miles distant' – every Saturday night, Saturday being market-day. Tess eventually begins to go too, and one day in September market and fair coincide. She looks about for her workmates – she fears going home alone – but finds most of them dancing. They are late leaving, and on the way home Tess gets involved in a row with Car Darch, one of Alec's mistresses, who is jealous of Alec's partiality for Tess. Many of the workpeople are drunk or tipsy, Tess edges away from the main group, and D'Urberville arrives on horseback to get her away. As Car's mother remarks, Tess has now gone 'Out of the frying-pan into the fire'.

Commentary

(See the section on *Writing and publication,* p.11). This is a most important chapter – the fate of the heroine and the narrative tension of the novel depend upon it. Note the effect of coincidence/fate throughout – Tess does not know that fair and market coincide, she meets Alec accidentally, she laughs at the treacle incident with Car Darch, thus bringing down the latter's wrath upon her. The description of the dancing is imbued with a kind of comic realism, particularly when the husband inadvertently brings his wife and others down. A range of Pagan references gives the scene a kind of mock-heroic quality. The agument between Car and Tess, preceded by the spilling of the treacle, again speaks of realism. We note that once again Alec appears opportunely and, as on the previous occasion, Tess is vulnerable and in no position to reject his offer. The women, particularly Car Darch's mother, act as a kind of Greek chorus on Tess's situation. The narrative speed and drama of the chapter is superb, from the leisurely beginning in innocent relaxation to the incidents and the climax with Tess carried off by Alec.

parish relief i.e. the care of the poor with its degrading economic basis – bitterly attacked earlier by Dickens in Oliver Twist.
weekly pilgrimages Ironically, the 'religious shrine' is the alehouse or the fair and market, or all of them.
'What – my Beauty?' Again, the phrase tends to make Alec melodramatic, larger than life.
overshoe i.e. the powder had come over their shoes.
satyrs clasping nymphs Rustic deities of classical mythology addicted to sensual pleasures. They worshipped Bacchus, the Roman God of wine, and the nymphs were minor rustic goddesses in the form of beautiful maidens.
Pans . . . Syrinxes Pan, the god of shepherds, huntsmen and country people; he pursued Syrinx, a Grecian nymph, who fled into the river Ladon. She was changed into a reed, from which Pan made his pipes.
Lotis . . . Priapus Lotis was a nymph who sought to escape the attentions of Priapus, the phallic god of fertility. She was changed into a shrub, the lotus. Note that for Tess pursued by Alec there is no escape, and that the invocation of classical contrasts here by Hardy is a deliberate way of underlining the fate of Tess.
Sileni The old companion of Bacchus frequently shown as a drunken and leering old man.
The Flower-de-Luce Fleur-de-Lys (iris, lily flower).
greased Loosened up.
turn Dance.

Queen of Spades ... Queen of Diamonds Aptly and contrastingly
named, the pick of a degraded pack – and we remember the 'trump
card' image of Tess's beauty.

a kind of rope In comic miniature this is symbolic of the hanging of
Tess.

queue i.e. pigtail.

black stream ... slimy snake Both description and image have an
ominous resonance suggestive of evil, and hence connect with Tess's
fate.

Our heroine ... Notice the proprietary tone adopted by the author at
the moment that Tess is about to be attacked.

th' beest everybody i.e. all in all (to Alec).

Praxitilean Praxiteles was the fourth century (BC) sculptor celebrated
for his statues of the goddess of love, Aphrodite.

rollicking Happy, joyful.

a horseman emerged Compare this with Alec's arrival in the gig on the
day that Tess leaves Marlott.

creepingly forward Note that this is a serpent image evocative of the
greatest of all tempters – Satan.

stroking her moustache Note the effect of this – it is at once comic and
grotesque (like the witches in *Macbeth*) and imitative of Alec's favourite
gesture when he is intent on conquest.

Chapter 11

Alec takes Tess out of the proper way and gets (temporarily) lost
near a wood as the fog comes down. Tess is naturally suspicious
of what is happening and does not trust Alec. The latter insists
that he is concerned for her safe passage back to Trantridge. He
steals a kiss from her, and makes a nest for her on dead leaves
while he finds out exactly where they are. Before that he tells her
that her father has a new horse that day. He has given it, and
Tess feels the more bound to him as a result. He finds out where
they are, returns to Tess, finds her lightly asleep but with a tear
on her lashes, and obviously rapes or seduces her. She is a
'maiden no more'.

Commentary

This is the climactic chapter of the first phase, with Alec at least
getting some response from Tess and playing his own 'trump
card' – the horse for her father – very well. Tess's object in
coming to Trantridge has been achieved, though she is to pay
the price almost immediately. Tess is exhausted, this being

almost an oblique reference to the long hours she works and the difference in social position between herself and Alec. Tess's physical pushing away of Alec is later undermined by his news of the horse. Alec makes her a nest (remember that she in inno-cence made a nest for Abraham), and the ensuing dialogue shows how near Tess is to surrender because of what he has done and despite her feelings of rejection for him. There is considerable omniscient commentary towards the end of the chapter, with particular reference to Tess's ancestors who doubtless seduced and raped when they felt like it. Hardy is here almost establishing the continuum of history and tradition, sum-med up in the local phrase 'It was to be.'

as into down The suggestion is of a vulnerable bird, the common image used of Tess, and it looks forward in a sense to her compassion later for the wounded vulnerable birds 'raped' by the hunters.

blackness Symbolic of evil.

the ironical Tishbite This is Elijah the Tishbite speaking to the priests of Baal when they called on their God (Kings 1, 18,27), the words being virtually quoted in the next lines here.

blank as snow i.e. white, undefiled, symbolic of innocence.

our heroine's personality Note again the proprietary tone of the author – from now on Tess will need defence.

Revision questions on Phase the First

1 Give some account of the Durbeyfield family and their reactions to the discovery of their family's ancient lineage.

2 With particular reference to any three of these chapters, say what impresses you most about Tess and why.

3 Write an essay on Hardy's use of humour in these chapters.

4 Write an account of the most dramatic or exciting incident in Phase the First.

5 In what ways does Alec D'Urberville appear to you to be a melodramatic or stage villain? You should refer closely to the text in your answer.

Phase the Second Chapter 12

Tess makes her way home carrying her belongings some four months after going to Trantridge. Alec catches up with her in his gig (note the contrast between her coming and her going) and offers to look after her, but she will not be his 'creature'. She parts from him in a cold manner, just acceding to his wish to kiss her. She arrives home, her mother being grossly disappointed that she hasn't got D'Urberville to marry her, and Joan blames Tess for thinking of herself. The injustice of this wounds Tess, who tells her mother rightly that 'I was a child when I left this house four months ago'.

Commentary

The immediate effect is that of contrast between Tess's coming and going, and the change in the dialogue between Tess and Alec will be noted too. Tess's misery is clearly evident (Hardy is very careful to document the exact passage of time) but D'Urberville still has some warmth and concern, even saying that 'if certain circumstances should arise' Tess may have 'by return whatever you require'. There is some fine natural imagery in this chapter, which is itself a comment on human nature, and we notice Tess's integrity and her refusal to tell a lie. Very significant is her meeting with the signpost painter, for both his texts relate – unconsciously but of course with telling structural force on the part of the author – to her state. The poignancy at the end of the chapter is almost unbearable, for Joan's cunning has no place in Tess's innocent way of life, and her daughter's words 'Why didn't you tell me there was danger in men-folk?' contain their own terrible indictment of Joan's hopes and manipulation.

late October . . . that day in June Hardy's chronology is meticulous, and the interested student can easly trace the time span of the novel.
the serpent hisses where the sweet birds sing Hardy no doubt has Shakespeare's *The Rape of Lucrece* in mind – 'The adder hisses where the sweet birds sing' – and the unquoted line which follows – 'What virtue breeds iniquity devours.'
She had no fear of him now . . . i.e. because she has already surrendered to him.
like a puppet The simple image stresses D'Urberville's lack of animation *and* also that she is the plaything of fate.
(of which he was to see more one day) An ominous anticipation of the murder.
as if you couldn't get a ribbon more than you earn A reminder – ironic – of Tess's wearing the red ribbon in her days of innocence.
'See how you've mastered me!' A direct echo of the 'kiss of mastery' D'Urberville gave her earlier (Chapter 8).

chill as the skin of the mushrooms . . . Another underlining
unobtrusively that Tess is constantly at one with nature.

my four months' cousin A considered ironic stress.

THY, DAMNATION, SLUMBERETH . . . This refers directly to Tess's 'sin' which
she cannot rid herself of later. In the manuscript of the novel Hardy
originally had THE, WAGES, OF, SIN, IS, DEATH.

**the last grotesque phase of a creed which had served mankind well in
its time** A perfect definition of Hardy's own agnosticism.

trade i.e. of one who has something to sell, here spiritual warnings.

THOU, SHALT, NOT, COMMIT- The Seventh Commandment is completed by
the word 'adultery' and thus refers to Tess's dilemma later, when in
desperation she feels that Alec, her seducer, is thus her real husband.

Mr Clare . . . Note how casually Angel's father is introduced into Tess's
consciousness – the irony being that she is never to meet him.

the handsome thing i.e. marry (Tess).

teave Strive.

dust and ashes An echo of the Burial Service ('ashes to ashes, dust to
dust'), and see Genesis 18,27.

fend Turn, set.

hontish Haughty.

Chapter 13

On the Sunday of her return Tess has visitors and Joan is
flattered by their attentions to Tess. But the latter withdraws
into herself more and more, and takes to going out after dark.
When she eventually attends church she knows that she is being
talked about. Hardy presents her as being close to nature despite
having broken a supposedly natural law.

Commentary

Tess is human enough to be cheered by her visitors, while her
mother's mood swings suddenly into a triumph over the flirtation
which might yet lead to marriage. Tess's mood too changes, and
she experiences extreme depression. When she goes to church she
is becomingly modest, but so sensitive that she spends her time
either in her bedroom with the children or communing with
nature. This communion with nature, Hardy says, with the moods
of nature corresponding to hers – 'midnight airs and gusts' produce 'bitter reproach' – leads her to a fallacy, 'a cloud of moral
hobgoblins by which she was terrified without reason. It was they
that were out of harmony with the actual world, not she.' Thus
Hardy asserts his faith in his 'pure woman'.

Robert South (1634–1716), the popular preacher of the Restoration period, the quotation being from one of his sermons

she could have hidden herself in a tomb Another unobtrusive link in the structural chain, looking forward to Angel placing Tess in the coffin (Chapter 37), and her lying on the altar at Stonehenge (Chapter 58).

'Langdon' The psalm-chant by Richard Langdon (1730–1803).

flexuous Full of curves (note the sensuality of the word).

the world is only a psychological phenomenon i.e. what we see as the world is related to our conceptions exclusively – Hardy follows this with 'what they seemed they were'.

Chapter 14

The chapter opens in the August of the following year, i.e. 14 months after Tess went to Trantridge, with a description of the sun and the reaping-machine. Tess has decided to join the harvesters, and her frail child is brought out by the other children so that she can feed it at lunch-time. But by the evening her baby is ill, so that as one grief goes 'a fresh one arose on the side of her which knew no social law'. Her father forbids her to send for the parson and Tess, obsessed by thoughts of hell-fire for her child if it is not baptized, rouses her brothers and sisters and baptizes the child Sorrow herself. The Vicar tells her later that it will be just the same as if he had baptized the child, but that he cannot give the child a Christian burial. It is buried in the shabby corner of the churchyard, Tess placing a home-made cross at the head of the grave and bunch of flowers in a marmalade jar at the foot.

Commentary

This moving chapter has Tess going from partial rehabilitation to great spiritual crisis. There is a fine focus on the sun and its life-giving qualities, but before we get to Tess there is a considered account of the reaping-machine and the inevitable death which awaits the small creatures who are left in its narrowing path. There is an unvoiced suggestion that Tess is trapped by the forces of nature in the same way, though here they operate through the insistent repetitiveness of Alec D'Urberville. The description of the field-women is poetic and lyrical, often in the graphic present to convey immediacy, though Tess works with 'clock-like monotony', which is almost an echo of the machine

itself and its demands which make for deadening monotony.
Note the considerateness of the men in not watching Tess feed
her baby, and also Tess's sudden transitions of mood which
reflect her insecurity, the consciousness of conflict between her
knowledge of her sin and her love for the baby later called
Sorrow the Undesired. She passes earlier through misery into
the courage of reappearance, and then into the apotheosis of the
baptism – this itself being one of the most moving sequences in
the book, with Tess almost taking on the colours of the Virgin
Mary. Her interview with the parson is significant, for he himself
is somewhat sceptical beneath his conformist exterior. The poignant exchange is made all the more so by its aftermath, the
burial of the child and the simple attentions of Tess. The incongruity of the marmalade jar in no way undermines the purity of
Tess's conduct, the simple faith which transcends both the pedantic and the ridiculous by virtue of its sincerity and humility.

heliolatries Modes of sun-worship, important reference here since
Tess has ventured forth into the sun (life). Angel is associated with the
sun in the novel and Tess is finally taken on the altar at Stonehenge,
where sacrifices were made to the sun.

like red-hot pokers Vivid sudden image, with again an emphasis on
the red.

Maltese cross i.e. having equal limbs, narrow where they join but
widening towards their extremities.

like the love-making of the grasshopper A fine capturing of the
mechanical effect.

the teeth of the unerring reaper A reminiscence of the sickle of Time
personified, but much quicker and more deadly.

holding the corn in an embrace like that of a lover The image is
tremulous with Tess's capacity for love which has been truncated by
her experience with Alec.

mid Might.

'A little more than persuading . . .' The suggestion is that Tess was
raped by Alec.

the maid who went to the merry green wood . . . An insight into rustic
humour, which is not cruel here but, as Hardy says, 'mischievous' and
without malice.

counterpoises Counterbalancing weights on the opposite side.

Aholah and Aholibah They would certainly make Tess more fearful,
since they were lewd (though Tess of course is not). It was prophesied
that they (and their children) would be put to death (Ezekiel 23).

quaint and curious details . . . in this Christian country Hardy's
scepticism makes him reject – using the omniscient voice – the extremes
of Christianity which assert the reality of Hell in the after-life.

a thick cable of twisted dark hair hanging ... An echo of Car Darch, and an anticipation of the rope.

immaculate beauty Note the adjective, which has religious overtones suggestive of purity, as in 'the immaculate conception'.

a phrase in the book of Genesis Jacob's wife Rachel died in childbirth, calling her child 'the son of my sorrow' (Genesis, 35,18).

stopt-diapason note The open diapason stop of an organ makes a grand swelling sound, and the stopt-diapason a somewhat softer sound.

by those who knew her ... This is an intimate identification with Tess, hence the warmth of the tone.

shone like a diamond The implication is of real worth – Tess is a pure jewel – but it looks forward ironically to the wedding-present diamonds, mere jewels compared to Tess.

Poor Sorrow's campaign ... the devil ... that fragile soldier A mixture of the Anglican baptisimal service and the concept of militant christianity typified by 'Onward Christian soldiers'.

begged Sissy to have another pretty baby Note the irony of their innocence.

ten years of endeavour ... actual scepticism No one knew better than Hardy the reality of the spiritual struggle to believe.

that shabby corner of God's allotment ... This superb rhetoric is really an assertion of Hardy's scepticism, perhaps best seen in the phrase 'conjecturally damned'.

little cross of two laths ... 'Keelwell's Marmalade' Here what is incongruous and grotesque is far from being funny – it is pathos of the highest and most moving order.

Chapter 15

Tess stays the winter months in her father's house, keeping a record of all the important dates in her last year or so and pondering on the time and place of her own death. She changes 'from simple girl to complex woman' through experience. She feels that she can never be fully comfortable again in her own village (though her story has been largely forgotten), and after waiting some time for a suitable opening she is told that a milkmaid is required for the summer months in a farm 'many miles to the southward'.

Commentary

Note Hardy's use of allusion as a form of commentary on the state of his leading character. Tess's pride is evident – she will not apply to Alec for money – while her natural morbid tendency (in part made worse by her experiences) is seen in her contemplation of her own death at some time. Her aloofness, her growing maturity and sensitivity, are all stressed, as well as her determination to 'annihilate' the past. She has some mystical hope of her new place – it is near her forefathers – and Tess is a girl of her time, superstitious, subject to changing moods. At the thought of going away she becomes almost optimistic, a telling contrast with her previous going away to Trantridge.

Roger Ascham A noted scholar of the mid-sixteenth century (1515–68), author of *The Scholemaster*, from which the thought quoted is taken.
Saint Augustine The greatest of the Latin fathers of the Church (354–430). The phrase is from his celebrated *Confessions*.
cramming Stuffing with food.
Jeremy Taylor's thought The reminiscence is from Jeremy Taylor's *Holy Dying*, a book of sacred eloquence. Taylor (1613–67) was probably a chaplain to Charles I during the Civil War.
like Babylon, had fallen Again we are aware of Tess's extreme (but understandable) sensitivity about her own fall, Babylon being synonymous with loose living and sexual license. Its fall is referred to in Revelations 14, 8, Isaiah 47 and Jeremiah 51.

Revision questions on Phase the Second

1 By close reference to the text, show that although Tess has broken a 'social law' she is in harmony with nature.

2 Write an account of the baptism of Sorrow, bringing out fully the pathos of the situation.

3 In what ways is Tess changed by her experience? You should refer closely to the text in your answer.

4 Give an account of Tess's reception by her family and friends on her return home.

5 Write a critical analysis of the scene between Tess and the parson and its aftermath. What does it reveal about the author?

Phase the Third Chapter 16

Tess leaves home 'two or three years after the return from Trantridge'. She passes the 'environs of Kingsbere' where her 'useless ancestors' were buried, but her spirits rise at the prospect before her. She sings, carried away by her mood, and eventually arrives at the dairy at afternoon milking-time.

Commentary

This is a transitional chapter, tracing Tess's move from Marlott to Talbothays as she enters a new 'phase' of existence. The journey, and her thoughts during the journey, are beautifully described and analysed, with the changes in Tess's mood traced sympathetically, from her rejection of her illustrious forebears to her contemplation of the colourful scenes of lands and cattle before her. Tess, now twenty, is 'mastered' (note the word) by the finding of this pleasure but, although she chants her praises she yet has a reservation (certainly Hardy's own) that 'perhaps I don't quite know the Lord as yet'. She finds expression for her feelings in the *Benedicite*, but she also feels the pagan influences within her. There is a fine natural contrast in the picturing of nature, the cattle being described in detail and with a fine colourful particularity.

On a thyme-scented, bird-hatching morning. . . Note the double-barrelled poetic effects which signal the change in Tess's circumstances.

useless ancestors Transferred epithet – they are 'useless' because dead, and anyway useless to her.

Van Alsloot or Sallaert Lesser-known Flemish painters of 17th-century country scenes.

the pure River of Life shown to the Evangelist See Revelation 22,1.

photosphere The visible surface of the sun.

before she had eaten of the tree of knowledge See Genesis 3 for the analogy with Eve.

'O ye Sun and Moon . . . for ever!' From the *Benedicite*, a canticle (song) which is part of the order for Morning Prayer in the Anglican *Book of Common Prayer*.

like a fly on a billiard-table A typical Hardy image to indicate natural perspective.

steading i.e. farmstead.

barton Farmyard.

milchers Cows to be milked.

Olympian shapes i.e. of the (Greek) gods who lived on Olympus.

Alexander, Caesar and the Pharoahs Ancient rulers of Greece, Rome and Egypt respectively.

as sandbags . . . like the legs of a gipsy's crock Commonplace images, but visually vivid.

Chapter 17

A description of the dairyman and of Tess's keenness to join in
the milking forthwith. The dairyman discusses the cows and tells
a story, and Tess discovers that one of the milkers is the young
man whom she had seen at the women's club-walking in Marlott
those years ago. Tess is temporarily dismayed for fear he should
recognize her – it also brings back the past from which she is
trying to escape – but he does not remember her. The other
milkmaids notice how pretty Tess is, and one of them insists on
telling her, though she is very tired, that the young man in
question is Mr Angel Clare, the son of a very earnest clergyman
of Emminster.

Commentary

Dairyman Crick is a talkative man, but kindly disposed towards
Tess (he is glad that another helper has arrived) and we see Tess
change from the serenity of her new job to fear of the past being
revealed – this is something which is to beset her on a number of
occasions at Talbothays. The description of the milking process
is meticulous, the dialogue between Jonathan Kail and Crick
humorous, while the story of William Dewy is both funny and
entertaining. It provokes Clare's first remark about the days
'when faith was a living thing', while some fine single word
effects describe the young man as he is – 'educated, reserved,
subtle, sad, differing'.

pattens Overshoes made of wood.
'pinner' Apron (worn by the milkers).
terminatively With finality, authority.
tay Tea.
kex Dry stem of a plant.
innerds i.e. insides.
nott Hornless.
bain't Are not.
lift up a stave Sing a song.
a cheerful ballad about a murderer . . . The terrible irony here is that
  Tess herself may become the subject of a ballad later.
Mellstock – William Dewy In Hardy's *Under the Greenwood Tree* (1872)
  William Dewy is the leader of the string (Mellstock) choir which
  accompanies the carol singers on Christmas Eve.
tranters Carriers.
seed Saw.
in the world i.e. in the morning.

leery Hungry, faint.
'Tivity Nativity.
clinked off like a long-dog Made off speedily like a greyhound.
leads Milk pans of lead.
wrings Cheese-presses.

Chapter 18

This is a filling in of detail on the Clare family and of Angel in particular, for he has refused to be ordained in the past. After years in 'desultory studies' Angel decides to go in for farming, and he is 26 when Tess re-meets him at Talbothays. He begins to take a delight in his companions and to love 'the outdoor life for its own sake'. He comes to appreciate the seasons, and one morning at breakfast he begins to notice the distinctive qualities of Tess. He thinks of her as 'a fresh and virginal daughter of Nature', and now remembers that he has seen her somewhere before, though he cannot think where.

Commentary

The retrospect on Clare shows his independence of view, though it is somewhat sententiously uttered as an attack on the church because 'she refused to liberate her mind from an untenable redemptive theolatry.' Despite his earnestness, we note the fixed position of Mr Clare, who believes one should work for 'the honour and glory of God', while his son believes in devoting himself to 'the honour and glory of man'. Angel's radicalism is mostly in the head, though we note that he was nearly 'entrapped by a woman much older than himself'. His idealism is anti-town life, and his education consists in gradually coming to love the ordinary dairy-workers and the country way of life. He becomes free from 'the chronic melancholy which is taking hold of the civilized races with the decline of belief in a beneficent Power' (though these views perhaps smack of Hardy more than Clare). There is a fine personification of nature – one of Hardy's great strengths – and Tess's registering with Clare shows him in responsive and sensitive mood. Her own statement that 'I do know that our souls can be made to go outside our bodies when we are alive' has a curious foretaste of the scene where Clare in his sleep carries Tess out to the coffin in his arms – his soul, so to speak, outside his body. The comparison of Crick's knife and fork 'like the beginning of a gallows' also carries a particular resonance in the text, for with Tess and Angel coming together, the movement towards the gallows does begin. There is the final irony of Angel seeing Tess as virginal, since the technicality of her virginity is to be so important to him later.

a system of philosophy Probably *On Liberty*, by John Stuart Mill (1806–73) in which he defended the rights of the individual. Echoes of it are found throughout Tess.

redemptive theolatry i.e. worship of God, belief in the redemption of man by God's sacrifice through Christ on the Cross.

theological thimble-riggers In the game of thimble-rig the conjuror conceals a pea under one of three thimbles, the onlookers having to guess which one it is under. The implication here is that many clergymen cheat by twisting the meaning of words to suit their beliefs. The phrase was coined by Leslie Stephen in his article 'Freethinking and Plain Speaking'.

Evangelical school A section of the Protestant faith which believes the essence of the gospel to be salvation by faith in atonement – a 'low church' section of the Church of England.

Indeed opine . . . Quoted from Robert Browning's *Easter-Day*, Section VIII.

Article Four Every Anglican clergyman had to subscribe to the Thirty-Nine Articles drawn up by the Church of England in the 16th century, the Fourth being the belief in the resurrection of Christ.

the Declaration The preface to the Articles (1562).

the removing of those things . . . The quotation is from Hebrews 12,27.

Hodge i.e. the personification of the countryman as simple plodding yokel.

The thoughts of Pascal . . . Pascal was the noted French philosopher (1623–62) whose *Pensées* are rightly celebrated. The quotation is from the preface, and translated reads 'The more imagination a man possesses, the more originality he is likely to find in others. Ordinary people do not find any difference between one man and another.'

Miltonic . . . Cromwellian The echo is of Gray's *Elegy Written in a Country Churchyard*:
> Some mute inglorious Milton here may rest,
> Some Cromwell, guiltless of his country's blood.

the road to dusty death From *Macbeth*, V, 5 – 'And all our yesterday's have lighted fools/The way to dusty death.'

Chapter 19

Tess and Angel get to know one another much better, being brought into close proximity through the milking. She hears

Angel playing the harp, but when he comes down into the garden she draws away from him. Their conversation reveals Tess's 'sad imaginings' to him, what Hardy calls in an omniscient aside 'the ache of modernism', but they do not fully understand each other. Angel is concerned at her bitterness. Later Tess asks Crick if Angel has any respect for the old county families, and learns of his radical rejection of people like her ancestors.

Commentary

Angel's 'ranging' of Tess's best milkers shows his interest in her, while his playing of the harp moves Tess, who is nothing if not sensitive, responsive and tremulous. The description of the garden is oppressively sexual, almost claustrophobic, with brilliantly imaginative associations, like 'The floating pollen seemed to be his notes made visible', while the remaining light is described as being 'like a piece of day left behind by accident'. Tess has a forecasting morbidity ('I'm coming; Beware of me!') which is borne out by events, and Angel sees that she is unusual indeed in her apprehensions and deep thoughts. Tess herself does not grasp Angel's own pessimism, but what is conveyed so well is their developing interest in each other. Tess has little confidence in herself with Angel, being, as Hardy puts it, unaware 'of her own vitality'. Angel appears, though perhaps not intentionally, condescending when he offers to teach Tess about history. It is poignant when she says that she wouldn't mind 'learning why – why the sun do shine on the just and the unjust alike', for here Hardy's heroine is underlining his own scepticism. The dismemberment of the 'lords and ladies' is a symbolic, superbly unconscious reflex attempt by Tess to rid herself of the rich family associations which have brought her into 'sin', and her questioning of Dairyman Crick is a pathetic attempt to find out the truth about Clare. She hears, of course, what Hardy calls 'this caricature of Clare's opinions', the irony being that she accepts it.

stealthily as a cat . . . cuckoo-spittle . . . thistle milk The whole
  sequence is evocative of Tess's sensuality and sexuality.
apple-blooth Apple-blossom.
hobble Anxious business.
Valley of Humiliation Christian passes through this in Bunyan's
  Pilgrim's Progress (1678).

the man of Uz See Job 7, 15–16.

Peter the Great in a shipwright's yard (1672-1725) The Russian
  Emperor worked in shipyards in Holland and England in 1697–8, and
  on his return began building the Russian Navy.

Abraham i.e. a man rich in cattle. See Genesis 12 and 13.

his spotted and his ring-straked Genesis 30, 25–43.

Andean altitude As high as the Andes, the great mountain range of
  South Amercia.

'lords and ladies' The popular name for the cuckoo-pint, obviously
  part of it being different coloured, and hence a lord or a lady.

Queen of Sheba See 1 Kings, 10. The Queen is overwhelmed by
  Solomon's splendour.

to know that I shall only act her part Tess is overtly stating her own
  fatalism.

on the just and on the unjust See Matthew 5,45.

niaiseries Foolishness (French).

rozums Eccentrics, people with odd views.

Chapter 20

Tess is now happier than she has ever been. She and Angel are
continually in one another's company, for they are the first to
rise, seeing nature in her various moods at close hand.

Commentary

This short chapter is lyrical with love, the love of Tess and Angel
and the love of nature. There is a closeness and a sense of
unalterable fate in the coming together of Tess and Angel, with
both of them impressed with 'a feeling of isolation as if they were
Adam and Eve'. The comparison is an ironic one since, as we
know, Tess has already tasted of the tree of knowledge. The
irony is further stressed through the religious and pagan references, while the descriptions of nature in its effects and in its
particularity – witness the herons with 'a great bold noise as of
opening doors and shutters' – are further enhanced by a succession of felicitous images – 'like a white sea' . . . 'like dangerous
rocks' . . . 'like glass rods' and 'like seed pearls'.

instalment Note the ironic force of the word which underlines the
  emphemeral nature of things.

convenances Conformities.

an irresistible law i.e. fate.

betimes Early.

the Resurrection hour. . .Magdalen Before dawn, Mary Magdalen
  being one of the three women, the 'fallen' woman blessed by Jesus.
  Tess is 'fallen' in the technical sense, hence the ironic biblical reference
  here.
Artemis, Demeter The Greek goddess of light and chastity and the
  Greek goddess of fruitfulness respectively.

Chapter 21

The failure of the butter to come in the churn leads to specul-
ation on the possible cause. There is the theory that someone in
the house is in love, and dairyman Crick tells the story of Jack
Dollop being trapped in the churn, a story which causes Tess
much unease since it bears some correspondence to her past.
She feels wretched for the rest of the day and goes to bed early.
When she is in bed and half asleep she hears the other
dairymaids talking about their love for Angel Clare. One of
them says that Clare prefers Tess, but Izz observes that he won't
marry any of them or Tess. The latter ponders on her love for
him and her situation.

Commentary

Local superstition is stressed in this chapter by reference to the
various 'conjurors', while the story itself is humorous and entertaining in the recital but not, alas, for Tess. The narrative cunningly has the milk start up again, which takes attention from
Tess. There is a fine examination of her inward consciousness –
and note the bleak correspondences with nature which reflect
her mood – and the sexual claustrophobia of the dairymaids'
chamber. Tess as inadvertent eavesdropper is 'deeper-
passioned', but her self-questioning is poignant with moral
indecision as to whether she ought to try to win Clare's love for
herself.

Conjuror A fortune-teller, one who practises country cures.
continnys Continues.
'hore's-bird A term of abuse.
Holy Thursday Maundy Thursday, the Thursday before Good Friday.
ballyragging Scolding vigorously.
pummy A mass of apples crushed to pulp.
make it right wi' her i.e. marry her.
dog-days The hottest days of summer, the time of the rising of the
  dog-star.

like a great inflamed wound in the sky A strongly visual way of
conveying Tess's misery.
machine-made tone Fine image to suggest the deadly monotony of life.
wi'en With him.

Chapter 22

The dairyman having been told that his butter has a tang, sees to
it that his employees scour the fields methodically to find the
offensive garlic. Tess and Angel work together and later drop
behind together. Tess draws his attention to the other milkmaids, and particularly to Retty, but she cannot do more than
this in her attempt to renounce Clare. From now on she tries to
avoid him.

Commentary

Tess's suffering continues, though Angel is unaware of it. Tess
does her best to interest Angel in the others, but although she
has plenty of courage in terms of motive she cannot long sustain
it in practice, since she loves Angel so much. The dialogue
reveals her heroism and, to a degree, Angel's insensitivity.

communistically An early use of the term, here indicating Angel's
determination to work and be treated in the same way as everybody
else.

Chapter 23

The four dairymaids walk to church after a downpour. A flood
prevents them from continuing along the lane, but Angel Clare,
who is not going to church, appears, and carries each one over in
turn, Tess being the last. It is quite obvious to the others that
Clare likes Tess best (he has also, unheard by them, assured Tess
that he does) though she asserts that they are better than she is.
When the four girls are together again the others realize that
their passion for Clare is hopeless. That night they can't sleep,
and one of them tells Tess that a lady has already been picked
out by his family for Angel. Tess now thinks that Angel's attentions to her are not of marked importance.

Commentary

The aftermath of the heavy thunderstorms creates an atmosphere in which the passions of the girls are heightened. There is a pathos too in the girls' concentration on Angel, all the more effective because he is unaware of them and interested only in Tess. The latter actually displays a sense of humour at the dilemma all of them are in, and this makes her radiant, though when Izz expresses her own trepidation and her self-indulgence in the arms of Clare we realize what Tess is in fact suffering. Again there is a certain humour in the exchange between the two girls. (Note that in the serial version Hardy negated the sexual overtones of the carrying scene by having the girls pushed in a wheelbarrow through the flood). A fine sense of contrast is achieved in the reactions of each of the girls. When it comes to her turn Tess, frightened at her own susceptibility to Angel, tries to draw back. She even affects to misunderstand something and this leads to an exclamation of love in all but words. Again there is a stress on fatalism, but equally effective is the kind of shared fever of the girls, proximity and that love combining to create an atmosphere of suppression because they sense the futility. Hardy phrases the feelings superbly when he refers to 'a killing joy'. The chapter again ends on a note of expectation when Tess learns that a lady has already been chosen for Clare.

Sun's-day i.e. sun-worship (despite the Christian association) which looks forward to the 'sacrifice' at Stonehenge.

Turnpike way i.e. where a turnpike (barrier) was operated across the road, users of that road having to pay a toll.

thistle-spud A pronged instrument for weeding out thistles.

sermons in stones Adapted from Shakespeare's *As You Like It*, Act II, Scene I, where Duke Senior is able to
Find tongues in trees, books in the running brooks,
Sermons in stones, and good in every thing.

A time to embrace... An echo of Ecclesiastes 3,1 and 3,5. The words apply poignantly to Tess.

Three Leahs to get one Rachel See Genesis 29 where Jacob is in love with Rachel, is promised her after seven years' work, is deceived and given Leah, but finally obtains Rachel.

I did not expect such an event... Tess affects to mean the flood – she really means being carried by Angel.

The poor child... This description of Retty reminds us that Tess was a child when she was seduced.

the thorny crown Another biblical echo, associated with the suffering of Christ.

Chapter 24

Out in the meads, milking in the hot days of summer, Angel Clare closely observes Tess and finds himself irresistibly attracted to her, so much so that he leaves his own pail and comes to take her in his arms. When he sees her in tears he is moved to say how devoted to her he is, 'signifying unconsciously that his heart had outrun his judgment'. Everything is changed for them from now on, though of course no one else knows of this.

Commentary

The atmosphere evocative of passionate love is established through a kind of concord with nature – the gad-fly torturing the cows, the blackbirds and thrushes retiring to the shade under the currant-bushes. Tess is the picture of quietness and meditation, but her flesh – and particularly her mouth and red top lip – drive Angel to distraction. Even here though there is 'the touch of the imperfect', almost as if Tess's feature mirrors the imperfection of her nature. Clare is sexually moved, almost for the first time, into action, and Tess's response shows her deep love and, at the same time, her fear. The inevitability is stressed once more.

Thermidorean Very hot (from the name of the month in the French Republican calendar beginning on 19 July).
Ethiopic i.e. from Ethiopea.
purled Flowed gently.
diurnal Daily.
keen as a cameo Note the vividness of outline which this implies.
red top lip The emphasis on 'red' again, reflective of passion and blood.
roses filled with snow Probably an echo of a line by Thomas Campion, the Elizabethan poet who wrote of lips that 'They look like rose-buds filled with snow'.
aura Sensation.

Revision questions on Phase the Third

1 Give an account of life at Talbothays Farm and Tess's part in it.

2 Write a character-sketch of Angel Clare as he appears so far.

3 Analyse two scenes in which Hardy's description of nature plays an important part.

4 Write a description of either (a) the three milkmaids or (b) Dairyman Crick.

5 Show how Hardy creates atmosphere in any of these chapters.

Phase the Fourth Chapter 25

Angel ponders on his situation now that he has fallen in love and wonders at the changes this has occasioned. He is aware of temptation in Tess's presence, and decides to go home for a few days. As he approaches the little town he sees Mercy Chant, the girl his parents had quietly hoped he would marry, and then at home his parents and brothers, all of whom are described in some detail. He realizes how far he has grown away from them, and they in turn see a change in him.

Commentary

Clare is in reaction to the emotion that has overtaken him, his passion for Tess which was not contained by his reason. He has also learned, at some expense to his self-image, that the unexpected can rule. There is a superb personification of the house which seems an advocate of his staying, and an omniscient comment which establishes the capacity for strong individual experience. Clare is here presented as a man of conscience, particularly in his relationship with Tess. In effect he withdraws, temporarily, from temptation; that withdrawal, together with its effect on the girls, almost forecasts his later withdrawal from Tess and the effect his marriage has immediately on the girls. Angel's inward debate gives way to the family descriptions noted above. Hardy's fine sense of contrast provides ironic detail, the brothers in particular being something of caricatures, while the religiosity of the family is stressed. The portrait of Mr Clare is detailed and, though it sufficiently indicates his bias, it notes his salient feature, sincerity. His kindness is above all differences. Angel's sensitivity, the effect of experience on him as distinct from theories or creeds, is given due prominence in the account of his reactions. The family appraisal, in turn, of Angel becoming more like a farmer, has the ring of truth. The brothers are limited, circumscribed by dogma and theory, presented satirically by Hardy as seen through Angel's eyes, and perhaps his own, particularly in their response to outward or cultural fashions. Angel has keen insight enough to know that 'neither saw or set forth life as it really was lived'. The dialogue with Angel has something of condescension in it, but the close of the chapter, with the firmness of Mrs Clare in using Mrs Crick's gifts of black-puddings and mead, is delightfully humorous at Clare's expense.

Walt Whitman American poet (1819–92), vigorous, humanitarian, controversial, the quotation being from *Crossing Brooklyn Ferry* (1856).

'pleasure girdled about with pain' An echo of two lines from Swinburne's poem *Atalanta in Calydon* (1865).

Antinomianism Faith in Christ is supreme and comes before the moral law.

court-patched with cow-droppings A humorous metaphor, since black patches of silk were worn by society women in the 17th and 18th centuries to enhance their complexions.

Wycliff, Huss, Luther, Calvin Famous Protestant reformers against the Catholic Church from Wycliff in the 14th century to Calvin in the 16th.

Conversionist This is exactly what it says – an enthusiast devoted to converting people to Christianity.

Timothy, Titus, Philemon All epistles of St Paul.

Christiad ... Paul iad i.e. St Paul's epistles were more significant than the gospels in Mr Clare's eyes.

Schopenhauer and Leopardi Schopenhauer (1788–1860), German philosopher, Leopardi (1738–1837), Italian poet, both noted for their pessimism.

Canons and Rubric i.e. the laws of church government and the rules for the conduct of divine service.

the Articles The Thirty-Nine Atrticles which all Anglican clergy must agree to observe.

geocentric view of things This is the idea, completely disproved, that the earthe centre of the universe.

nymhs and swains Terms used in the pastoral tradition of poetry, and hence ionic here.

Wordsworth ... Shelley The great romantic poets of the early 19th century, Wordsworth (1770–1850) the poet of nature, Shelley (1792–1822), passionately radical genius.

Correggio (1494–1534), Italian painter who produced several studies the Holy Family.

Velasquez The great Spanish painter (1599–1660).

Diocesan Synod and Visitations The dioceses of the Church of England which organized the administration; the higher clergy conducted visitations to the parishes in a supervisory capacity.

dapes inemptae Unbought feasts (Latin).

delirium tremens A delirium, with horrifying delusions, suffered by heavy drinkers (Latin).

pretty tipple Good drink.

Chapter 26

Angel gets an opportunity to speak to his father about Tess and, while unable to lay aside their prejudices in favour of Mercy Chant, at least his parents do not object to meeting her. He praises Tess, assuring his parents that she is sound in her Christian views. He sets off for Talbothays, his father accompanying him a little way on the road and telling Angel of an abusive encounter he has had with a renegade young man – Alec D'Urberville. Clare is appalled by what his father has to put up with.

Commentary

Angel, for all his unorthodoxy, obviously wishes to have his parents' approval in marrying someone out of his class. The Clares' advocacy of Mercy Chant shows their religious limitations, and further underlines the distance between parents and son. The chapter is inlaid with irony, since what Angel says of Tess shows his apparent enlightenment – it is only apparent until he is put to the real test later. The mention of Alec D'Urberville and the incident is essential to the plot, since it adds to the irony and looks forward to the unlikeliest sequence of all – the conversion of Alec D'Urberville – the likeliest aspect of this being his re-temptation by Tess. Angel's reaction to this shows that he is unworldly, while his father, as we would expect, is unostentatiously sincere and courageous.

your goings-out and your comings-in See Psalm 121, 'the Lord will watch over your coming and going.'

with flowers and other stuff This fashion spread after 1847 in the area, perhaps being typical of the High Church manifestation of the Oxford Movement of the 1840s.

flummery Nonsense.

Pauline i.e. after St Paul.

epiderm Outer skin.

Calvinistic Intolerant (see note on Calvin p.52).

its ghostly legend of the coach-and-four Typical of Hardy's structural sense that this legend, which is central to the idea of fate and inheritance in the novel, should be referred to here with the 'fateful' mention of Alec D'Urberville.

'exclaim against their own succession' See *Hamlet*, Act II, Scene 2, line 375.

'Being reviled we bless. . .' 1 Corinthians, 4, 12–13.

pietist i.e. excessive piety.

in the position of poor parsons for the term of their activities Strictly speaking this is not true – Cuthbert is a Fellow and Dean of his Cambridge College, comfortable enough to marry Mercy Chant, as we learn later in Chapter 57.

Chapter 27

When Clare gets back to Talbothays he quickly asks Tess to marry him. She, shaken and oppressed by her sense of guilt, refuses, citing his family position as an excuse, while admitting her love for him. Clare thinks that he has been too precipitate with her, and goes on to undermine her confidence (unconsciously) still further by referring to his father's brush with an unnamed cynic whom Tess recognizes as Alec D'Urberville.

Commentary

Clare's sensitivity, even complacency, is shown in his viewing Talbothays as he approaches it from a perspective which he knows his parents could not have. The somnolence of the afternoon is stressed, and Tess yawning is given a natural physicality and voluptuousness which Clare can't resist. Descriptions of her add to her sensuous appeal – ironically innocent in intention – like 'she was as warm as a sunned cat'. Tess is greatly moved but courageously sticks to her sense of honour and, pressed by Clare, has the honesty to admit of her church-going that 'I wish I could fix my mind on what I hear more firmly than I do . . . It is often a great sorrow to me.' But the drama of the chapter is that as Tess grows 'serener' Angel's story regarding his father has unconsciously reinforced her refusal.

like half-closed umbrellas A typical Hardy image, visually apt.

the red interior of her mouth as if it had been a snake's A fine mixed image, indicative of the good and (supposed) evil in Tess.

Tractarian The High Church practices which resulted from the *Tracts*

for the Times (1833–41) written by John Henry Newman (who later
joined the Catholic church) and John Keble among others.
Pantheistic Pantheism sees the manifestation of God in all things.
Many of Wordsworth's poems are good examples of this.
Leave thou thy sister... The verse is quoted from Tennyson's *In
Memoriam* (1850).

Chapter 28

Angel continues to question Tess about the reasons for her
refusal, since he knows that she loves him. She in her turn
communes with herself, wishing that someone had told Angel of
her transgression. He persuades her to give him a final answer
on the following Sunday. Tess is oppressed by the fact that,
because she loves him so much, she feels that she will find herself
'drifting into acquiescence'.

Commentary

The dialogue between the lovers is convincing, Clare being
moved to a passion which seems to be greater because it is being
resisted. There is also the irony of his not knowing anything of
her past, and thus feeling that she already has encouraged him
by admitting his advances. We marvel at the nobility of Tess's
character as she continues to repulse him for his own good, as
she puts it, despite her love for him. As she rightly tells him, 'you
don't know'. There is a further irony in her wishing that someone else will tell Angel the truth about her, while the other girls
and Dairyman Crick remain tactfully quiet yet know that the two
are in love. Angel's kissing her vein is the sign of his passion, his
harvesting of her, so to speak, in the apposite image where she is
compared to 'a sheaf of susceptibilities'. Notice how she is
wounded by the charge of coquettishness, but how her mood
sways, so that she considers she may 'snatch ripe pleasure before
the iron teeth of pain would have time to shut upon her', a
superb animal-trap evocative of Tess's natural instinctual being
and suffering as victim. She is too overwrought to go to the
afternoon milking, and her sensitive nature endures much self-
torment.

to make love to her i.e. admit his attentions.
trowing Knowing.
'sigh gratis' Sigh hopelessly.
an establishment i.e. marriage and a home.

the first urban water i.e. the implication is that she is sophisticated and experienced.

spotless There is a terrible irony in Clare's use of the word in view of his ignorance about her past.

a great forge in the heavens A fine pictorial image, almost with the effect of a painting.

Chapter 29

The dairyman recalls his tale of Jack Dollop (which so embarrassed Tess) by bringing the story up to date. He has married a widow for her money, but she has lost that money on her remarriage, much to his dismay. Tess is among those who say that the woman ought to have 'told him the true state of things – or else refused him', a remark terribly appropriate to her own situation with Angel. When Angel follows her out, she continues to refuse him, the tale having given her strength; Clare coaxes her, and one morning after she has called him presses the question. She realizes that she will have to give in, the opportunity occurring later when Clare asks her to accompany him to the station with the milk.

Commentary

Again the anecdote reveals Tess's susceptibility, her own superstitious and highly imaginative nature which causes her to identify with like situations in others. There is humour in the story, but if there is one distinct limitation in Tess it is that her own sense of humour is not a developed one. Hardy puts it superbly when he observes 'What was comedy to them was tragedy to her.' There is an ominous reference to the future which shows Hardy's careful structuring, when Clare puts his arm 'beneath her hanging tail of hair', an innocent anticipation of the rope. Angel's not kissing her in fact saves her from committing herself to him, one of Hardy's casual might-have-beens in the development of events. We notice Angel's cunning, moving from passion to coaxing, so that Tess is 'softened up', but this seems natural in Angel in view of her very obvious attractions. Their exchange between three and four in the morning shows Tess in all her unconsciously provocative sexuality. She tells Angel that the other girls are better than she is, typical of her guilt feelings and generosity of spirit. Clare reveals his opportunism in asking Tess to accompany him and, it must be admitted, some insensitivity in view of the fact that she is not dressed for a journey at night.

riddling i.e. as if he is asking a riddle.
beright i.e. by rights.
the ghost of her first man This is precisely Tess's situation now, and accounts for her discomposure.
just before they went to church Tess, of course, tells Angel after the ceremony on their wedding evening.
scram Puny, weak.
crosses Tess bears her own cross, and arguably later is influenced at the Cross-in Hand.
self-immolation i.e. killing herself.

Chapter 30

Tess and Angel are absorbed in each other, despite the rain falling upon them, though Clare protects them both with a piece of sail-cloth. On their way to the station they pass the D'Urberville mansion and Tess tries to tell Angel of her past, prefixing it with the fact that she is a D'Urberville. Clare immediately jumps to the conclusion that this is all her trouble, and Tess faintly agrees. Clare reacts positively to the news and is in fact pleased by it. Tess in her weakness and love agrees to marry him, and Clare realizes that he has seen her before – on the green. Tess hopes that the fact that he did not dance with her then will not prove to be an ill-omen.

Commentary

Descriptions of nature and of Tess are the prelude to Angel's proposal, with the D'Urberville mansion providing one of those forecasting or associated moments which are symbolically placed at crisis points in Tess's experience. The rain too is in sympathy with Tess's mood, which is not enhanced by the D'Urberville reference. It is, however, typical of her courage that, although she turns the conversation towards London and their milk being drunk there, she recurs to her D'Urberville ancestry as the direct way into her confession. That confession is partial; Tess, forever human, tremulous and vulnerable, and very much in love, cannot complete it. Note Clare's snobbery when it comes to marrying a D'Urberville, despite his disclaimer about rank, even to the point of his calling her Teresa as well as urging her to take her old name. Tess's anguish is terribly conveyed by the 'dry hard sobbing', her passion and its quality by her kissing Clare. We feel that he is not equal to her and not her equal. The memory of his having seen her in all its vagueness is perhaps emphatic of the different intensity of their natures.

like battlemented towers . . . The fanciful image is consonant with Tess's imagination *and* the mansion they are soon to pass.

mirrors of light . . . sheets of lead Notice that these changes are reflected in Tess's changes of mood.

Caroline In the time of Charles I (1625–49).

a friendly leopard at pause Another cat image which expresses Tess's unawakened sexuality.

centurions Tess is in error – they were commanders in the ancient Roman army, and hence this is an anachronism which Angel repeats ironically.

mushroom millionaries i.e. those who have grown to prosperity quickly.

lucubrations Laborious night study.

Chapter 31

Tess receives a letter from her mother in response to one she has written in which the latter urges her not to mention her past trouble. Tess puts the past as far as she can out of her mind, but delays the wedding day too. She considers that Clare is all goodness, and one evening when they stay in, Tess bursts out that she is not good enough for him, and wishes he had stayed with her four years ago when they had met in passing on the green. Clare announces their engagement to the Cricks, and when she gets back to her bedroom Marian, Retty and Izz stand round her. Tess breaks into 'a hysterical fit of tears' but is comforted by the others; Marian is particularly generous.

Commentary

Tess is ashamed of her mother's letter, which is a semi-literate piece of self-interest – again Joan has failed her daughter. Tess idealizes Clare, so much so that she herself 'seemed to be wearing a crown'. Hardy's own comment on Clare provides a balancing emphasis – 'he was, in truth, more spiritual than animal'. The idyllic nature of their existence is seen against nature, though again Tess is compared to 'a wary animal', an indication perhaps that she is on the defensive all the while. Clare uses a phrase used by Joan of Tess earlier, saying of Tess's D'Urberville ancestry that 'It is a grand card to play'. This shows Hardy's structural awareness again. Tess's own joy is undermined from time to time, and here a strong animal image is used, for the 'gloomy spectres' of 'doubt, fear, moodiness' were 'waiting like wolves'. Clare inadvertently brings on her outburst by praising her and telling her that she is 'of good report', something that bites into her conscience. Hardy records her anguish, and that she was 'caught during her days of immaturity like a bird in a springe'. Tess's natural modesty is shown when the Cricks enter, for she disappears quickly. The interaction with the other girls is both dramatic and poignant, for they are 'like a row of avenging ghosts' yet their sympathetic associations with Tess, despite their own sufferings, are strong, for 'she do live like we'. In a terrible sense their kindness causes Tess more suffering since it accentuates her own sense of unworthiness because of her wrong.

J write these few lines Notice how Hardy has captured Joan's character and practice in print by having her write *part* of her letter in the third person.

wearing a crown i.e. like a queen, not the crown of thorns.

Byronic . . . Shelleyan i.e. like the romantic heroes of Byron or Byron himself (1788–1824) or having the more ethereal and imaginative quality of Shelley (1792–1822).

a grand card to play A deliberate echo of Joan's 'trump' card in relation to Tess's beauty.

photosphere The luminous envelope of sun or star from which its light and heat radiate.

of good report Note the irony of the phrase, and its immediate effect on Tess.

springe Trap.

on my own hook i.e. independently.

like an elastic ball Note the speed and flexibility of the image.

baily Bailiff.

Chapter 32

The wedding-day is still not settled by the beginning of November, and Angel Clare remarks that Tess's services may not be required at the farm after Christmas. Tess is finally brought to name the day, the last day of the year, and writes to her mother to tell her and again to ask for advice. Clare makes their plans – he wishes to see the working of a flour-mill – but one day Izz tells Tess that the banns have not been called. This is because Angel has arranged for the wedding by special licence. Angel has clothes sent from London for Tess.

Commentary

The natural background is described, and there is one remarkable manifestation when 'From the whole extent of the invisible vale came a multitudinous intonation' as if of a city, noted by Tess, unheeded by Clare. The quality of her imagination and susceptibility is stressed here. Clare speaks – it is a measure of a kind of insensitivity – of carrying Tess off after marriage 'as my property'. The decision made, Tess becomes passive, a natural response after the strain she has been under. What she does note, however, and this reveals her practicality, is that it might have been better for Angel to have been settled in a job before they got married. Note Angel's snobbery, and his sense of his wife's 'trump' card (in his sense) in his choice of the lodgings in the mansion that had been 'a branch of the D'Urberville family'. Tess continues full of foreboding; one terrible phrase conveys it – 'All this good fortune may be scourged out of me afterwards by a lot of ill' – and when she stands in front of the mirror, her mother's 'ballad of the mystic robe' comes back to her.

the red rising up Symbolic of embarrassment, passion – and blood.
bolting Sifting.
called home i.e. had her banns proclaimed.
That never would become that wife ... Queen Guenever The extract is from a ballad called 'The Boy and the Mantle'. It is as described by Tess here, Guinevere being King Arthur's wife.

Chapter 33

Angel and Tess spend Christmas Eve shopping in the town. Tess is recognized by a Trantridge man who insults her; Clare hits him, the man withdraws, and later that night Clare has a dream in which he pummels his portmanteau in mistake for the man.

Tess puts a note under Clare's door containing her confession but the next day Clare seems unchanged to her and, on the wedding day, Tess goes up to the room and finds the letter unopened under the carpet. She wants to confess to Clare but he won't have it. They drive to the church in an old carriage. Tess is oppressed, thinking that she has seen the carriage before. Clare tells her something of the D'Urberville coach legend, and she is even more oppressed. They are seen off on their honeymoon by all at the dairy, Clare kissing the girls goodbye at Tess's request. As they leave the cock crows towards Clare.

Commentary

This oppressive chapter is full of omens, with the legend of the D'Urberville coach and the cock crowing foremost among them. The man's insult brings Tess's past back forcibly to her, Clare's dream prefigures his later one after their marriage, while the letter not being read by Clare illustrates the part played by fate. There is an effective contrast between the non-attendance of Angel's family and the warmth of the Cricks' preparations for the marriage, while all the time we are aware of the milkmaids in the background, each nursing her forlorn love. Clare is rather complacently aware of Tess's real rank, and once again the image, here of the 'grand card', is used to show his future plans. Tess's suffering through the fact that she has still not confessed is almost unbearable. By inclining herself towards him in church Tess shows both the depth of her love and her insecurity. She intuitively knows that Clare loves her image rather than her, and the chapter ends with a distinct feeling of unease after the crowing of the cock.

blower A hanging over the fireplace, designed to produce an upward draught.
gieing Giving.
randy Party.
bass-viols Violoncellos.
temerarious i.e. impudent.
partie carrée Group of two men and two women.
louvred Of turret-like shape, with overlapping boards to admit air but not rain.
like the angel whom St John saw in the sun See Revelation 19,17.
I seem to have seen this carriage before . . . This adds a mystical dimension to Tess's morbidity and imagination.

Is it when we are going to die ...? Again, Tess is near to the truth of
her own later case – but notice Angel's tactlessness in even broaching
the subject.

Friar Laurence ... In Shakespeare's *Romeo and Juliet*, Act II, Scene 5 –
these are in fact much quoted words.

for she you love is not my real self, but one in my image This
poignant statement in actual fact reveals Tess's fears which Angel
translates into just these terms.

the crowing of a cock ... Peter denied Christ (Luke 22,60–2), but the
local superstition is that the bride is not a virgin. There is a terrible
irony – by not speaking Tess has 'denied' Clare, and Clare is later to
'deny' her when she does speak.

Chapter 34

Clare takes Tess to 'one of your ancestral mansions', but two
portraits of horrid women – both recognizably ancestors of Tess
– chill her, yet she and Angel mingle fingers under water as they
wash. Afterwards Clare contemplates her with love, while outside the weather changes. Inside Clare notices that his wife is
unsettled, but a special messenger brings a present of jewellery
from Angel's late godmother for his bride. Tess takes the jewels
and puts them on, Angel telling her to adjust her bodice so as to
set them off. Tess is greatly excited, and after supper Jonathan
Kail arrives with the news that Retty has tried to drown herself,
Marian has been found dead drunk, and Izz is in a thoroughly
depressed state. Angel tells Tess not to be depressed, and soon
confides in her of his own sinfulness in the past. The way is
opened for Tess at last, and she tells him her secret.

Commentary

Clare's tactlessness – his own inherent snobbery – is shown in his
choice of the decayed D'Urberville mansion for the honeymoon.
The D'Urberville portraits are rather stagey symbols to indicate
the evil lurking in the family. The mingling of Angel's and
Tess's fingers is the natural precursor to what should be sexual
consummation on their marriage night, but here it is ironic in
view of Angel's coming rejection of Tess. There are other ominous hints at what is to come, like the sun making 'a spot like a
paint-mark set upon her', symbolizing in miniature her sin.
Angel's inward monologue in which he considers that he will
never hurt Tess carries the now familiar irony, and another

image where she 'winced like a wounded animal' shows Tess's suffering at his 'I wonder if you really love me, after all?' Tess's donning of the diamonds makes her a real D'Urberville, and the scene is charged with sexuality, though Hardy wrily observes that 'fine feathers make fine birds'. Jonathan Kail's narrative further depresses Tess, and she shows the depths of her courage when she is about to tell Angel. She is forestalled by Angel's own confession and, deluded in her faith (and this is her tragedy), thinks that 'He seemed to be her double'. He isn't and, accompanied by ominous description, she begins her own tale.

it was too near a satire Clare's sensitivity shows here but it is really too late.

their being builded into the wall Ironic that they, like Tess, are trapped.

a spot like a paint-mark Note the mixture of blood, guilt, and the reminiscence of the paint-pot man who painted the scriptural texts on the walls.

the restful dead leaves of the preceding autumn ... resurrection Note how this natural phenomenon is equivalent to the movement of Tess's conscience.

how to tuck in the upper edge of her bodice Notice the strong sexual overtone here, ironic in view of the non-consummation to come.

a monotonous acreage of turnips on a dull day An unobtrusive anticipation of Tess's bleak experiences at Flintcomb Ash.

a jerk in the fire-smoke ... some giant had laid his hand Note again the relationship of this casual incident to Tess, the smoke coming into the room the quivalent of the guilt of her past being revealed.

gallied Scared.

mane Mean.

so to name what she lawful is Note the irony of this – Tess is a wife in law but not in fact.

mops and brooms from what's inside 'em Become intoxicated.

fetched Came.

trencher-woman Eater, having a hearty appetite.

traps Personal belongings.

night-rail i.e. night-clothes.

Aldebaran ... Sirius Bright flashing stars, the first the eye of Taurus the Bull, the second the brightest star in the heavens, also called the Dogstar.

He seemed to be her double A superbly economic way of conveying Tess's wish-fulfilment that she and Angel feel alike – the irony is that they don't.

spotlessness Note the emphasis, in view of the coming revelation the 'spot'.

Be thou an example ... See 1 Timothy, 4,12.

'Integer vitae' The quotation here and the two lines which follow are from Horace, the Latin poet, Ode I. The phrase means 'spotless life'.

a certain place Proverbial – 'The road to hell is paved with good intentions.'

a Last Day luridness in this red-coaled glow This is the end of the world and its consumption by fire according to Christian belief – more specifically it is the end of the world for Tess.

a sinister wink like a toad's The comparison somehow conveys the ominous results of her confession.

Revision questions on Phase the Fourth

1 Give some account of Angel's visit to his parents, indicating what it reveals of his character.

2 Analyse Tess's dilemma in relation to Angel, tracing clearly her feelings and her attempts to confess the past.

3 By referring closely to the text, indicate the part played by various omens in these chapters.

4 Write an essay on Hardy's use of nature in these chapters.

Phase the Fifth Chapter 35

It takes some time for what Tess has said to sink in to Clare. When it does he says that he regards her as another person, and Tess realizes that her own apprehensions have been fulfilled. She is distracted, and after further words Angel leaves the room. Tess follows him, and although he says that he will not reproach her, he does. They wander about that night, until Angel tells her to return to the house and go to bed. She dutifully obeys, and later that night Clare also goes back to the house. He hears Tess sleeping deeply, and goes to sleep himself on the sofa.

Commentary

The onset of change in human relationships is here imaginatively connected to the *supposed* changes in the fire and the fender, for example, but Clare's suffering is immediately apparent in his listless stirring of the fire and the fact that his face has withered. The opening words show that 'the depths remained paralyzed', and Angel cannot forgive – the difference in quality between the man and the woman is here apparent.

The laughter shows his inward hysteria. The contrast between Tess and Angel is marked, for she will accept anything he says or does, but he cannot accept the like in her. Yet Clare is moved to compassion by her suffering. Despite this, his sense of self obtrudes, and Tess is forced to follow him out, almost like a servant, 'with dumb and vacant fidelity'. Although he acknowledges that she was 'more sinned against than sinning' his lack of true social and moral perspective is calculated – perhaps unconsciously – to wound her when he says (and he was so proud of her ancestry) that she is 'the belated seedling of an effete aristocracy'. So overwrought is she that she contemplates suicide, and when she returns there is the bough of mistletoe to mock the aridity of their marriage. On Clare's return there is the portrait with the low bodice to mock him, and as he ponders we are aware of his smallness of view, of spirit, of mind in his contemplation of the wife who has been true in the ultimate sense – she has hidden nothing despite her own loss.

The fire . . . The fender . . . Note the effectiveness, in terms of atmosphere, of these personifications.
treadled i.e. moved his feet mechanically.
prestidigitation Trick. Note the pedantic, intellectual use of the word, which would be outside Tess's comprehension.
another woman like me . . . There is a terrible pathos in this – Clare has been in love with an image, not a reality.
good-hussif Needle and thread bag.
Agape Love-feast, hence ironic here.
Behold, when thy face is made bare . . . From Swinburne's verse tragedy, *Atalanta in Calydon*.
'I am only a peasant by position, not by nature!' Moving and explicit words which only call forth a reproach from Clare.
Cistercian abbey Probably Bindon Abbey, founded in 1172.
tester Canopy.
passion's slave See *Hamlet*, III, Scene 2.
The little less, and what worlds away! From Robert Browning's *By the Fire-side*, verse 39.

Chapter 36

Clare gets breakfast the next morning, and when they meet begs Tess to deny what she said. She can't, and naively suggests divorce. Repulsed again, she recurs to her idea of suicide, but promises not to contemplate it. Angel goes off to his work at the miller's, and, when he returns for lunch, is somewhat annoyed to find Tess working so hard. He forces her to accept the idea of parting, and in the meantime they live mechanically together. Tess eventually solves matters for Angel by suggesting that she should go home.

Commentary

Again the personification of the furniture contributes to the hopelessness of the atmosphere. Clare tries to lose himself in practical activity, but there is no escaping his own bias. There is pathos in Tess sitting so long in her bedroom, anguish in her 'purity', unwitting insensitivity in Angel's feeling that he deserved to secure innocence. It is difficult to accept Angel's (again albeit unconscious) condescension to Tess, but his concern at her working so hard shows that his humanity – and love – is trying to break through. It can't because, in Hardy words, there is in him 'a hard logical deposit, like a vein of metal in a soft loam'. A superb biblical echo ('she sought not her own') spells out the difference in emotional and human quality between Tess and Clare. His rejection of her proffered kiss symbolizes his rejection of her, but Clare is always a man of conscience, though sometimes misguided, and wishes that he had kissed her. He lacks the character, the integrity, to accept Tess for what she is, loving, repentant, pure in intention. His small-mindedness is shown in his thinking that her sin will be known everywhere. In fact Tess solves his problem by saying she will go home – and in ironic reply Clare says that he thinks better of people when he is away from them. This in fact proves to be true, but – another echo of the original title of the novel – it will be 'too late'.

as though associated with crime A comment on Clare's narrowness – in his own mind he has been contaminated.

It was with the cord of my box... A terrible irony in the fact that Tess considers killing herself in this way when she is later to be hanged.

she sought not her own... 1 Corinthians 13,5.

M. Sully Prudhomme The French poet and critic (1839–1907) who shared with Hardy a quality of pessimism.

fiat Order, directive.

knoweth not only its own bitterness See Proverbs 14,10 ('Each heart knows its own bitterness').

We do not say it Note the use of the omniscient voice to establish that there are two sides to every question.

somewhen Some day.
boreal Northern.

Chapter 37

Angel enters Tess's bedroom walking in his sleep. In his dream he imagines that Tess is dead, and carries her outside, placing her in an empty stone coffin in the ruined Abbey church. At first Tess had thought that he was going to drown her in the swiftly-flowing stream. She manages to humour him back and induces him to lie down on his own sofa-bed. She does not mention what has happened the next morning. The next day they visit the Cricks on the way to their separate lives. Tess goes to say good-bye to her favourite cows, and afterwards Angel gives Tess a sum of money and tells the coachman where to drive her. He wishes that she would look out of the window at him, but she is lying in a dead faint inside.

Commentary

This is one of the most stimulating, moving and upsetting sequences in the novel. Tess is at first joyful, thinking her husband has come to make love to her and completely forgive her, but this gives way to fear on his account – as ever – when she sees that he is asleep. Her trust is stressed. Clare is obviously acting out in his sleep a wish fulfilment – that Tess should be dead so that he will not have to bear the burden of her. The funereal references even before the placing in the coffin bear this out – she is wrapped in a sheet 'as in a shroud', he carries her 'with as much respect as one would show to a dead body'. The 'dead! dead!' and the 'So sweet, so good, so true' have echoes of Lear and Cordelia, and Tess has the kisses which are denied her in the day. Angel is thus revealing his deeper love and his divisions within – he loves her but does not wish to love her, preferring in his sub-conscious that she should be dead. The account is filled with narrative tension as we fear – as Tess fears – that Angel may awake. Tess rightly connects his dream with the action in the past when he carried her and the other dairymaids, but the present is fraught with danger as he crosses the unsafe bridge, plus Tess's fear, and ours, that Angel may be about to drown her. Tess even wishes that they should die together. This gives way to her guiding of Angel – ironically something that she cannot do in life – for the aftermath of the dream is Clare's cold wish that they should separate. Notice the immediate effect on the already overcast atmosphere of the seasonal changes at Talbothays, plus the humour at Tess's expense and the story of Marian and Retty. All this contributes to Tess's sadness. The behaviour of Tess and Angel is finely defined by Mrs Crick when she observes 'they stood like waxen images and talked as if they were in a dream!' The parting is evidence of Angel's fixity of purpose and of his rationality – only his dream has released his emotions. And even in the parting the contrast is marked, for Hardy notes if Tess had made a scene Angel would probably not have been able to stand out against her.

beatific Used ironically in view of its religious connotations.
he fancied she had risen as a spirit The phrase recalls Tess's own idea of ghosts outside the body – the first words which caused Angel to notice her.
like a Samson shaking himself See Judges 16,20.
fiasco Complete failure.
the fly The carriage.
the fury of fastidiousness At first the phrase seems a paradox, but it exactly fits Clare's emotional attachment to principle.
God's *not* in his heaven . . . A deliberate ambiguity on Hardy's part, for the words are Clare's and express his mood, but they also express Hardy's views in a much more permanent sense. The *two* lines are from Browning's 'Pippa Passes' – 'God's in his heaven/All's right with the world.'

Chapter 38

Tess goes home, tells her mother that she told Angel the truth, and gets very little sympathy. Her mother in fact calls her a 'little fool', and when Joan conveys the news to her husband his main concern seems to be his own loss of face, since he has been bragging about the marriage to his drinking companions. He even doubts whether Clare has married her. Tess overhears all this and, when she gets a letter from Clare saying that he has gone to look at a farm in the North of England, she makes this the excuse for leaving home, first giving her mother twenty-five of the fifty pounds that Clare has given her. She feels some pride in this, making Clare appear a generous husband in her parents' eyes.

Commentary

Tess's learning of her father's drinking on account of her marriage is a further source of distress to her, and this is so strong
that she goes towards the house by a back lane. The dialogue
with her mother rings true, Joan's selfishness and irrespon-
sibility are well to the fore, Tess's sensitivity and anguish in her
love for Clare too much for her mother to comprehend. Tess is
further made to feel her unwantedness when she realizes that
she no longer has a bed, and her overhearing what is said
between her mother and father is overlaid by the irony that her
father had wished her to take the name 'D'Urberville' on her
marriage. Notice how the chapter ends on a note of deception,
Mrs Durbeyfield thinking that husband and wife are reconciled.

'Nation Damnation.
what's done can't be undone See *Macbeth*, Act V, Scene 1; the punning
  on 'done' and 'undone' runs throughout the play.
unceiled Unplastered.
glane Sneer.

Chapter 39

Clare's state of mind is described. He visits his home, surprising
his parents by the fact that he has not brought his wife. He tells
them that she has gone home and that he intends to set out for
Brazil. Questioned about her, he insists that she is 'Pure and
virtuous'. Mr Clare reads from Proverbs in praise of a virtuous
wife and, still further questioned by his mother, Angel insists
that his wife is spotless. But he is still conventional in his heart.
Meanwhile, Tess thinks 'how great and good her husband was'.

Commentary

Clare, despite his intellectual acceptance of what he has done,
finds himself disturbed by the situation. He now lacks the will to
pursue his farming studies. He even reasons that he has
deserved this result because Tess is a D'Urberville, which reflects
how irrational Clare can be. At the same time he wonders if he
has treated her unfairly, and snatches at Brazil – after all, what
she has done will not be known there. But there is great power
and forthrightness and praiseworthy dishonesty in his insistence
that Tess is pure to his mother. The reading from Proverbs is

riddled with irony, the more so for being given at some length, but the 'blind magnanimity' which he recognizes in his mother is even more terrifying in its dealing with improvements that Clare can make in his untutored wife. Hardy puts Tess's case unequivocally when he observes of woman generally that her moral value has 'to be reckoned not by achievement but by tendency'. Clare's limitations are fully exposed in this chapter.

like a ghost an echo of his dream and of Tess's early words.

Wiertz Museum Named after the morbid Belgian painter Anton Joseph Wiertz (1806–65). His studio in Brussels later became a museum.

Van Beers (1852–1927) A portrait painter whose work Hardy probably saw when he visited Brussels.

the Pagan moralist A quote from Marcus Aurelius (121–180), Roman philosophical writer.

the Nazarene Jesus, here a quote from John 14, 27.

the Empire of Brazil Here Hardy is using material within living memory, *The Times* having reported (1872) the troubles of the British emigrants who had been promised a farming career in Brazil but succumbed to its climate and diseases.

as the dive of the kingfisher A fine natural image, but one can't help feeling that it is somewhat ironic in view of Angel's personality.

a good thing could come out of Nazareth See John, 1,46. ('Can there any good thing come out of Nazareth?')

The words of King Lemuel ... Proverbs 31,1.

neither the world, the flesh, nor the devil A reminiscence of the baptismal service.

her moral value having to be reckoned not by achievement but by tendency This is the key to Hardy's theme in the novel.

Chapter 40

Clare meets Mercy Chant and, in his unhappy mood, whispers to her 'the most heterodox ideas he could think of'. He thinks he is going mad. After that he pays thirty pounds into the bank and goes on to the Wellbridge farmhouse, where he had spent that short time with Tess. He finds the mistletoe still there, bemoans the loss of Tess, and meets Izz Huett, who gives him bad news of Marian and Retty. In an impulsive moment he asks Izz to accompany him to Brazil; she agrees, but Angel thinks better of it when she tells him how truly Tess loves him. Izz suffers greatly when he is gone. Five days later he leaves for Brazil.

Commentary

The whole emphasis is on the waywardness of Angel's moods – his teasing of Mercy being insensitive, his doubts of his sanity, his anguish at the loss of Tess, his complete lack of consideration in taking advantage of Izz's love for him to ask her to be his mistress. The moral Angel Clare is in abeyance and, and this is where the weakness and the egoism of the man are so striking. It still lies with him to contact Tess. But Angel is obdurate, and the might-have-been of reconciliation is sacrificed to the sheer bloody-mindedness of emigration

His momentary laughter . . . Indicative of Clare's unbalanced mood.
The mistletoe hung under the tester The symbolic effect of this is central to the suffering of Clare and Tess – it indicates the might-have-been, indeed the should-have-been of their marriage.
no great things Not much good.
She would have laid down her life for 'ee 'That a man lay down his life for his friends' John 15,13.
Like the prophet on the top of Peor See Numbers 23, 13–24.
poor little act of justice to an absent one? Note that Angel himself does not match Izz's generosity in his treatment of Tess.
as a dying man to the dying The Nonconformist preacher Richard Baxter (1615–91) wrote of 'a dying man to dying men', but Clare's words here are melodramatic, imbued with self.
a feather-weight's turn i.e. very close to.

Chapter 41

Eight months later Tess is looking for work, and has had to fall back on some of the money Clare has given her. She has to give some to her parents to repair the thatch of their house. During this period Clare has become critically ill from fever in Brazil. Tess sets out for a farm in the middle of the county which Marian has told her of by letter, and on her way meets the man whom Angel assaulted before their wedding. She takes to her heels, and spends the night in a wood, being somewhat disturbed by the noises around her. The next morning she finds that these have been made by the wounded pheasants, and she puts as many of them as she can out of their misery.

Commentary

Tess's 'utter stagnation' of mind is stressed during her long period of light work, and there is a degree of pathos in her parting with Angel's precious sovereigns – precious primarily because he has put them into her hands. Typically she gives most of what is coming to her to relieve her parents' distress. So strong is her conscience that she puts away from her any thought of money being raised on the jewels (though she doesn't know where Clare has deposited them). Structurally we notice that Clare's suffering parallels Tess's, almost as if his decision is responsible for both their situations. Her pride is evident in seeking employment away from places where she is known, and there is also concern that her husband's reputation should not suffer from their separation. Note Marian's generosity in writing to her, and the now common comparison of Tess to a wild animal. She stoically endures insults, but when she meets the man from Trantridge she becomes desperate, thinks – ironically – of her husband being in a 'warm clime' – and spends the night restlessly. When she identifies the strange noises Tess, with a rare courage, 'killed the birds tenderly'; the action is typical of her character, her ability to see other suffering as greater than her own. Yet in a terrible way this action forecasts the later action of murder, here from compassion, later from hate – hate at being deceived. Again we are aware of Hardy's sense of structure.

éclat Dashing success.

Black Care An echo of Horace's 'Black Care mounts behind the horseman'.

the habitude of the wild animal By now this is a common image of Tess, expressive of her freedom and innocence – and also of her as a victim.

Angel had knocked down ... Perhaps a small error by Hardy, for the man was not knocked down but merely staggered.

making a sort of nest in the middle A phrase riddled with irony – remember that Alec had made Tess a nest for the seduction.

All is vanity See Ecclesiastes 1,2 (the words were spoken by Solomon).

a sort of gasp or gurgle The connection is obvious – the echo is of struggle for survival which approximates to Tess's.

their rich plumage dabbled with blood ... feebly twitching a wing Note again the immediate connections with Tess.

accoutred Dressed.

like the inhabitants of the Malay Peninsula This is factually correct and a striking indictment of man's inhumanity to wild life, something about which Hardy felt very strongly.

Chapter 42

Tess presses on and, being the object of unwelcome attentions, cuts off her eyebrows and puts on her oldest field gown to make herself plain. Her long journey in suffering eventually ends when she gets to a cottage, leaning against its wall for warmth. She has arrived at Flintcomb-Ash, and meets Marian; she is taken on by the farmer's wife until Old Lady Day.

Commentary

The poignancy is Tess's suffering, but she is sustained by a rare courage and determination in her attempts 'to despise opinion', though these are undermined by forward young men. When she hears herself unflatteringly referred to she grits her teeth; Hardy makes her fortitude and suffering all the more graphic by going into the present tense ('Thus Tess walks on . . .') The plateau is described in strongly sexual terms, almost in contrast to Tess and to her present sterile state. Fittingly, the bleak village of Flintcomb-Ash is located in 'a slight depression'. The moment of supreme pathos comes when we are told that 'The wall seemed to be the only friend she had'. Notice that Tess is so reduced that she is glad to see a Marian who has obviously degraded herself and who in different circumstances Tess would not have cared to meet. The simplicity of their dialogue is at once apparent, and so is Marian's warmth. It is ironic that Tess does not see the farmer who would, of course, have recognized her.

mommet Ridiculous figure.
The maiden's mouth is cold From Swinburne's 'Fragoletta' verse 9, the
  first line of which begins 'Ah sweet, the maiden's mouth is cold'.
Cybele the Many-breasted This analogy was not in the manuscript of
  the novel. She is the Greek nature goddess, the many-breasts being
  suggestive of her fertility function.
plashed down Bent down.
tilt-bonnet Sun-bonnet.
clipsed or colled Hugged and embraced.
Old Lady-Day 6 April, the quarterday before the change in the calendar
  in 1752. Thereafter Lady Day became 25 March, but often the old date
  was observed on contracts.

Chapter 43

Tess works in the swede-field with Marian, who points out to her the place of Talbothays in the perspective. Things are somewhat relieved by Marian's coarse sense of humour, and she says that she will get in touch with Izz and Retty. The winter is a very severe one, and during it Izz joins them. The two 'Amazonian sisters' who were involved in the Chaseborough incident are working there but do not recognize Tess; the farmer, the Trantridge man assaulted by Clare, does. Tess works hard at the reed-drawing, and Marian is moved to tell her that Angel had asked Izz to go off with him to Brazil. Tess, typically, though crying, blames herself but not Angel.

Commentary

There is fine atmospheric description of the bleakness of situation which approximates to the bleakness of mood in Tess. The latter is sustained by patience. There is an analogy drawn between Tess and the landscape – 'it was a complexion without features, as if a face, from chin to brow, should be only an expanse of skin.' In effect there is a strong indictment of piece-work payments built into the account of both the outside and the inside work. The recurrence to Talbothays is natural in view of their deprived circumstances, and Marian's turning to the bottle contrasts with Tess's fortitude, the irony being that Marian of course does not know the truth about Tess and Angel. The chapter is physical in its graphic presentation of the cold and its effects, a fine image indicating the stealthy onset of winter 'like the moves of a chess-player'. There is a strong sense of identity, of perspective and of beauty in Hardy's description of the strange birds which come there, and of the arrival of the snow. A brilliant image almost forecasts Stonehenge in the penultimate chapter, when the roof is described as 'a gymnasium of all the winds'. There is a strong dramatic effect in the presence of Car Darch and the Queen of Diamonds (indicative of the evil past), the arrival of Izz (the happy past) and the presence of the Farmer (the discovered past), all contributing to Hardy's sense of structure. Tess forces herself to behave in a dignified manner, conscious of her status as Mrs Angel Clare, but there is pathos in her effort. There is greater pathos still when, after the revelation that Angel had asked Izz to accompany him, Tess that night wears her wedding-ring next to her heart.

lanchets or lynchets Beds of flint.

siliceous Quartz.

cusped Pointed.

some early Italian conception of the two Marys In Italian art a
representation of the Virgin Mary and of Mary Magdalene.

gaunt spectral creatures with tragical eyes Notice how the birds in
some ways approximate to Tess, again emphasizing her oneness with
nature.

Aurora Aurora borealis, the northern lights, a luminous meteoric
phenomenon seen in the sky towards the Polar regions.

reed-drawing Separating straws for thatching roofs.

like a bird caught in a clap-net Again the simile emphasizes the fact
that Tess has been and is often trapped. The clap-net closes when the
string is pulled.

thirtover, lackaday Obstinately lazy.

Chapter 44

Tess is moved to think of Clare's parents as she longs for news of
him. Their wedding anniversary approaches, and one Sunday
morning Tess sets out very early to walk the fifteen miles to
Emminster. She calls at the Vicarage but finds no one at home,
since they are all at church. She sees Mercy Chant and recognizes Angel's two brothers, one of whom finds Tess's thick walking boots which she had deposited in a hedge. Their
conversation discourages her, and she turns back, regarding her
meeting with them as an ill-omen. On the way back home she
stops in a village to get some refreshment. She is told of a ranter
preaching there; when she goes to see him out of curiosity she
finds that it is Alec D'Urberville.

Commentary

The worries about Angel which move Tess to pay the visit to his
parents are clearly stated. Vivid imagery still stresses the
extreme cold ('the ground ringing under her feet like an anvil')
and the pathos continues with her dressing up prettily to meet
them. There is a considered use of symbol, later to take on a
greater importance, with the association of the Cross-in-Hand –
'the site of a miracle, or murder, or both'. The boots are also
symbolic, Tess's pathetic idea of looking nice for her in-laws by
discarding them capped by the ungenerous interpretation of
their having been left by a vagrant by her 'Christian' rival Mercy

Chant. Little wonder that Tess is oppressed by her visit, that her superstitious nature responds to the overheard coldness of those 'to her – super-fine clerics'. We are in her consciousness at this stage; more, we share the author's irony at the might-have-been, the fact that had she but known it Mr and Mrs Clare would have given her the sympathy she needed. But if the coincidence – always bulking large in Hardy – of her seeing Mercy Chant and the brothers is marked, even more remarkable is the recognition of Alec D'Urberville. Fate, indeed, seems to hold all the trump cards, to adapt Joan Durbeyfield's image to her daughter's situation.

steely starlight without and the yellow candlelight within Indicates Tess's situation between warmth and happiness on the one hand and coldness and loneliness on the other.
hogs'-backs Hill-ridges shaped like pigs' backs.
beating up Overtaking.
guindée Stiff, strained (French).
quizzing Interpretation.
Publicans and Sinners ... Scribes and Pharisees Publicans were tax-gatherers and grouped with sinners in St Matthew's Gospel, while the Scribes and Pharisees represent strict and formal righteousness which was censured by Christ.
ranter Rhetorical, shouting preacher who declaims his text, much associated with the Nonconformists.
O foolish Galatians ... Galatians 3,1.

Revision questions on Phase the Fifth

1 Compare and contrast the attitudes of Angel and Tess to their situation.

2 Write an essay to show that Hardy's choice of title for this section – 'The Woman Pays' – is relevant to the narrative in these chapters.

3 How important are journeys in these chapters? You should refer closely to the text in your answer.

4 Write an essay on Hardy's use of imagery in this section.

5 In what ways does coincidence play an important part in this section?

6 Describe life at Flintcomb-Ash as it is shown in this section.

Phase the Sixth Chapter 45

When Tess moves Alec recognizes her and loses his powers of speech. She walks away as fast as she can, but he follows her and overtakes her when his service is over. He gives her some account of his conversion, which he lays at the door of one Mr Clare. Tess does not believe in his getting religion, and he responds to Tess's beauty, which he regards as temptation. He is struck mute when she tells him of their baby, and makes her swear on the Cross-in-Hand that she will never tempt him. When he leaves her he reads over Parson Clare's letter to him. Meanwhile Tess goes on her way and finds Izz Huett being courted by Amby Seedling.

Commentary

The initial emphasis is on Tess's reaction to the physical transformation of Alec, and also to the incongruity of his speaking religious words. In a fine paragraph Hardy himself spells out the 'transfiguration' and its contrast with the past, a contrast emphasized by the antithetical balances in the style – 'good new words in bad old notes' and 'The greater the sinner the greater the saint.' D'Urberville's paralysis is dramatic, his following of Tess equally so, his words matching his passionate temper. The terrible irony of his being converted by Mr Clare contributes to the interaction between himself and Tess, for she has just come from not seeing Mr Clare, though having experienced in her own mind the un-Christian reactions of his sons. There is too irony in the fact that Alec believes himself converted Tess can't accept the suddenness of it, while we are certainly in doubt, since his following Tess is an index to his passions. The onset of sexual feeling in Alec is apparent when he tells Tess 'Don't look at me like that.' Such is the strength of temptation that he forces Tess to swear on the Cross-in-Hand, the stone perhaps being symbolic of what she has had to and will have to bear. D'Urberville is perturbed after the meeting, Tess greatly agitated when she meets the labouring man who tells her that a malefactor 'was tortured there by nailing his hand to a post and afterwards hung'. Again we are aware of the forecasting nature of this – Tess has in effect nailed her own hand at Alec's command, and it will lead to her hanging. Her meeting with Izz is charged with pathos – Tess, too, might have been innocently courting – in fact did, with Angel – had she not met Alec in the past.

rencounter Meeting.

Paganism Paulinism The comparison is obvious and, ironically, stresses the change in Alec which echoes the differences in Mr Clare and Angel.

her Cyprian image Physical love, from the goddess Aphrodite, the Greek deity worshipped in the Eastern Mediterranean and especially Cyprus.

she wished not to encounter alone on this side of the grave Another forecasting death association with Tess.

the old Adam i.e. the sinful man.

'Come out from among them . . . See 2 Corinthians, 6,17.

bitter and black with sorrow Tess's simple language unconsciously made more tragic by the reference to the baptismal name of her dead child.

wuld Old.

petite mort Literally little death, shock (French).

Chapter 46

Tess works in the fields in 'joyless monotony', and Alec, having brooded on the situation, comes to see her. He tells her that his mother is dead and he intends to become a missionary; he also wishes to marry Tess and has bought the licence. She tells him that she loves somebody else and also that she is married. He becomes progressively more emotional, being particularly moved by her eyes. He taxes her with the absence of her husband and the nature of that husband, seizes her hand, but they are interrupted by Farmer Groby. Tess begins a letter to Angel; Alec appears again at the cottage, continues to harass Tess and misses a preaching engagement at Casterbridge Fair. His 'backsliding', as he calls it, has begun.

Commentary

Irony runs throughout the chapter with the offer of marriage coming 'too late' and in any case unwanted by Tess. The scene, in its bleakness, is calculated to undermine Tess's resistance, and Alec goes the right way about it by his genuine concern for her situation, though his feelings are described as 'capricious compunction'. It is incongruous when Alec suspects that the labourer with whom Tess is working may be the man in Tess's life. The exchanges between Alec and Tess are imbued with their feelings – natural dialogue – and it is to Alec's credit that he expresses a wish to help Tess and her husband. He immediately undoes this generous thought by his opportunism in seizing Tess's hand. The exchange with Groby effectively underlines Tess's reactions, for she dreads her 'defender' (Alec) more than her 'assailant' (Farmer Groby). The extent of Tess's undermining by her experience with Alec is shown in her failing to finish the letter to Clare. D'Urberville's visit to her lodging is dramatic, and Tess in telling him the views which she has absorbed from Angel undermines d'Urberville's own newly-discovered Christianity, thus strengthening his determination to have her. Death imagery emphasizes his loss of faith.

wales Narrow bands.

and devote myself to missionary work in Africa Ironically, like Angel's sister.

Angels of heaven! Notice that in this exclamation Alec inadvertently, unknowingly, invokes 'angels', the one 'Angel' having behaved in a singularly unheavenly way to Tess.

'Od rot i.e. God curse.

Candlemas Fair 2 February, a festival of the Catholic Church in honour of the purification of the Virgin Mary.

the Sermon on the Mount See Matthew, 5, 3–12.

Dictionaire Philosophique The philosophical work by Voltaire (1694–1778) first published in 1764, noted for its scepticism.

Huxley's *Essays* T. H. Huxley (1825–95) the scientist who coined the word 'agnostic'.

'servants of corruption' 2 Peter, 2, 19–20.

witch of Babylon Revelation, 17,5 – 'The Mother of Prostitutes'.

Chapter 47

On a March morning the threshing of the last wheat-rick at Flintcomb-Ash begins. Tess has one of the worst jobs, has no respite, and at dinner-time realizes that D'Urberville is there watching her. She remains at the top of the rick, though it is cold and windy. D'Urberville comes up to tell her that he has abandoned the religious life. He gets nowhere with Tess, who strikes him on the mouth with her glove when he insults Angel. Alec tells her that if she is anyone's wife she is his, and that he will return that afternoon to get her answer about her going away with him.

Commentary

Notice the atmosphere immediately and the treatment of the working women The threshing machine is given a considered male personification which somehow makes it a threat, almost identifiable with Alec in some ways, but expressive perhaps of Hardy's resentment of tradition being encroached upon by machinery. The impersonality and itinerancy of the engine man are also stressed. The placing of Tess on the platform of the machine is a piece of sadism on the part of Groby. The exhausting nature of the work is described, the dialogue between Marian and Izz natural and unforced, they being the first to note the restoration of Alec D'Urberville, now dressed as he used to dress. Tess is, literally, trapped between man and machine – in this threshing scene she is typically victim. Alec is as sexually drawn towards her as ever, as he reveals when he mentions the effect her figure has on him. Tess is emotional herself and cannot really communicate with Alec in a rational way, and Alec delights in throwing back her husband's words in her face, since they are responsible for his rejection of religion, though he certainly uses a religious reference to Hosea in order to win her over. The passionate swing with the glove is prefigurative of murder, and shows Tess's own passionate and impetuous nature. She herself observes 'Once victim, always victim – that's the law!', a statement definitive of her own situation and of her own and Hardy's fatalism. Tess, with her supersititous response to moral law, is virtually compelled by two things here – the fact that Alec was once her master, and what she would see as justice in his assertion 'If you are any man's wife you are mine!'

the red tyrant A phrase evocative of blood.

primum mobile First mover (Latin).

Tophet See particularly 2 Kings, 23,10. It was Hinnom near Jerusalem in the Old Testament, the place for human sacrifice and the burning of idols, and hence synonymous with Hell.

Plutonic Infernal, Pluto being the Greek God of the Underworld.

autochthonous Of the earliest inhabitants.

hev Has.

the seven thunders See Revelation, 10, 3–4.

het Gulp.

hagrode Tormented.

Weltlust Love of sensual pleasure (German).

a strong puritanical stream ... The religious channel is left dry forthwith The image contrasts strongly with Tess's own 'religious channel' in the moving baptism of Sorrow.

Hymanaeus and Alexander See 1 Timothy, 1, 19–20. They were both handed over to Satan in order to teach them not to blaspheme.

the bachelor-apostle Probably St Paul.

skimmer-cake A thick pancake.
A scarlet oozing . . . blood A prefiguring of the effects of the murder.
the sparrow's gaze before its captor twists its neck Another bird image
  for Tess, who is to be the final victim when she is hanged.

Chapter 48

Alec comes back in the afternoon, tries to help Tess, treats her
politely, walks to her lodgings with her after her long and tiring
day, and offers to assist her and her struggling family. Although
she is tempted to accept help for her family, she decides that she
can take nothing. Alec's own religious mania is over. That night
Tess writes a long imploring letter to her husband, letting him
know that she is being subjected to the pressures of temptation.

Commentary

As the outdoor scene draws to a close there is some fine descrip-
tive imagery, the faces of the threshers being dyed 'with a coppery
light', but the focus is on Tess and her near-physical exhaustion,
an exhaustion which duplicates her earlier fatigue when she was
seduced by Alec. She is frightened to leave for fear of Alec, but
after the killing of the rats – a mixture of comedy and certain
distaste here – she does so, even acknowledging that Alec has
perhaps meant to be kind. D'Urberville plays on her feelings for
her family, and the letter that she writes to Clare is a cry for help,
impassioned, poignant, deeply-moving, for she is conscious of
her own temptation in her run-down and poor state.

nammet-time Mid-morning or mid-afternoon snack.
the long red elevator like a Jacob's ladder See Genesis, 28, 10–13.
Pandemonium See Book I of Milton's *Paradise Lost* (1667), where
  Pandemonium is the capital of Hell, the abode of demons, in which the
  Fallen Angels hold their council.
as a bled calf Another animal image of Tess, reminiscent of her
  seduction and the birth of her child.
I don't like to see the rooks and starlings . . . Tess is turning away from
  nature because she is so overwrought at her plight.

Chapter 49

Tess's letter arrives at the parsonage and is duly directed on to
Angel, both parents being inclined to blame themselves over

Angel and his marriage. Meanwhile Angel's sufferings and those of his fellow emigrants are shown, together with the effect on his thinking of his treatment of Tess. One man in particular tells him that he has been wrong, and after his companion's death he begins to see this, so that 'from being her critic he grew to be her advocate'. He begins to value her ancestry, while Tess, after her outpouring to him, practises the ballads that she knows that he likes, weeping the while at her lost love. Just before she is due to leave, Liza-Lu arrives with the news that her mother is dying, and Tess sets off for home.

Commentary

This is a linking chapter, comparing and contrasting Clare and Tess in their separation and different experiences. We note the sensitivity, even if somewhat misplaced, of Mr and Mrs Clare, and the fact that Angel has had to travel thousands of miles in order to appreciate his own narrowness of vision and the real worth of Tess. The account of Angel's experiences is graphic; in the structure of the novel, the burial of the child by the mother is equivalent to Tess's suffering over Sorrow. Angel comes to appreciate that it is the 'aims and impulses' which are the real morality, that his own views have been parochial until he was enlightened by the 'large-minded stranger'. Tess's devotion is seen through the ballads, the one quoted having a terrible pathos and poignancy. The chapter ends dramatically; notice that Tess is still appealed to, that she is, in effect, the centre of this decayed and decadent family.

as Abraham might have mourned . . . Genesis, 22, 1–14. Abraham has been told by God to sacrifice his son Issac, though this is later reversed.
Hellenic Paganism i.e. Angel has elevated the ideas and ideals of ancient Greek civilization.
Tess would lay down her life for him See Izz Huett's words to Angel in Chapter 40.
aura Atmosphere.
Was not the gleaming of the grapes of Ephraim . . . See Judges 8, 1–3.
It would have melted the heart of a stone . . . This is a platitude now, but here an effective image to indicate the *depth* of Tess's love.
traipsing Wandering.
drave Compare 'slave and drave', that is, toil.
withy basket i.e. made of strips of wood.

Chapter 50

Tess walks through the night and, reaching home, takes on all the cares of her parents' household, outdoors and in. One evening she is working on the family allotment when, after a long time, she notices that Alec D'Urberville is working beside her. Once again she turns down his offer of assistance. Tess's father, not her mother, dies, and with his life the lease of their cottage is terminated. What has happened to the Durbeyfields doubtless happened to those who were tenants of the D'Urbervilles in the past.

Commentary

Tess is in many ways a novel of journeys, and this one undertaken by Tess is significant in terms of the plot. Notice that as she goes her imagination carries her into other houses and takes her back to the past when she had first seen Angel on the village green. John Durbeyfield's money-making project is a further underlining of the family's deprivation, but Tess, as we should expect, rises to the occasion by her practical activity, or, as she feels, 'Violent motion relieved thought.' There is something melodramatic about the appearance of Alec D'Urberville unnoticed by Tess because of her self-absorption, though the constant association of him with the tempter, the devil, is here reinforced by the grotesqueness. Fate, however, continues to dog Tess, and the unexpected death of her father means that the pressures Alec can bring to bear – like caring for her family – are calculated to undermine her resistance.

pricked and ducked i.e. pricked with needles and ducked in the pond.
'whickered' Sniggered.
'pillar of a cloud' See Exodus, 13, 21 – 'the Lord went before them by day in a pillar of cloud.'
Jupiter The largest planet of the solar system.
that scene of Milton's ... *Paradise Lost*, Book IX, 626–7, 629–31, where Satan is intent upon tempting Eve to eat of the Tree of Knowledge. Alec enjoys playing the part.
'liviers' i.e. those tenants who occupied their homes for as long as they lived.

Chapter 51

Tess and the family have to leave – Tess's sin in the past now being unfavourably commented on – intending to seek lodgings in

Kingsbere which, in their mother's view, is the family seat. Alec D'Urberville calls and offers Tess a cottage for her family; although she refuses, her mind is sorely torn, and she writes an agonized letter to Angel in which she accuses him of being 'cruel, cruel indeed!' and says that she will try to forget him. On the last night in their house she persuades the children to sing songs, but when her mother returns she says that her husband will never come. She is now beginning to believe that Alec, her seducer, is her real husband.

Commentary

There is some social comment in the account of the enforced movements of agricultural labourers and their families on Old Lady Day, Hardy waxing somewhat bitter about the migrations towards the towns as 'the tendency of water to flow uphill when forced by machinery'. He also comments on village morality. Tess contemplates the dead spider, which is a symbol of herself as victim (like the spider, she has been misplaced), though the next symbol, that of the legend of the D'Urberville coach, is introduced by Alec. Tess is further tried by Alec's offer, since her family responsibility has been increased by the death of her father, and their poverty and enforced move is lowering to her spirits. She is further tempted, since Alec offers guarantees, but her releasing of the stay-bar is another indication of her impetuosity, a prefiguring of her capacity for murder. Her letter to Angel shows the state to which she has been reduced. The song of the children embodies the idea seen early in the novel that their lives are blighted, while the quotation from Wordsworth is seen by the omniscient author as satire rather than faith.

Egypt ... Land of Promise See Exodus, in which the story is told of how the Israelites escaped from slavery in Egypt and set out for the Promised Land.
Here we suffer grief and pain From a Sunday school song published in 1832 which became very popular.
Not in utter nakedness ... Lines taken from Wordsworth's (1770–1850) *Ode on Intimations of Immortality from Recollections of Early Childhood*, the next line being 'From God, who is our home'. Hardy as we have seen earlier, is opposed to Wordsworth's ideas.

Chapter 52

The waggon comes for the Durbeyfields' goods, and they see many other waggons on the road on this fateful day. Tess meets Marian and Izz, who tell her that Alec has called at Flintcomb to enquire after her. The Durbeyfields' situation worsens when they learn on their arrival at Kingsbere that the rooms they were to have have been let because their letter was delayed. The furniture is unloaded under a churchyard wall, near where the mansion of the D'Urbervilles had stood in recent times. Tess's mother regards the D'Urberville family vault as freehold. Alec D'Urberville appears in the midst of the unloading, Tess having gone into the church. She enters 'her ancestral sepulchre', Alec follows her, seeming to her to be an effigy that moved. He leaves, but Tess wishes that she were dead. Meantime Izz and Marian have driven on. They determine to write to Angel Clare to warn him of an enemy's temptation of Tess, and they send the letter to Emminster vicarage.

Commentary

It is stressed that Tess and her mother are 'only women', and therefore they get no farmer's help in their removal. The meeting with Marian and Izz is fortuitous – the letter at the end of the chapter is expressive of their good-heartedness – and the making of a nest for the children reminds us of other 'nests' in the novel which have been close to tragedy. Tess's death-wish is very apparent here, and the fact that the family are in their own family of D'Urbervilles, so to speak, carries the unspoken irony that just as those fell, so they have fallen too. Alec is enjoying his following of Tess. Humanity speaks very directly through Izz and Marian's action in writing.

house ridding i.e. moving of goods.
Ark of the Covenant The sacred chest containing the covenant between God and the people of Israel who carried it on their journey to the Promised Land. (Exodus 25)
stale Urinate.
martin-holes i.e. made by sand-martins.
Ostium sepulchri . . . 'The door of the sepulchre of the ancient D'Urberville family'.
their land of Canaan See note on 'Egypt' in Chapter 51.
The old order changeth A quotation from Tennyson's *Morte D'Arthur*.

tole Lure.

Stone . . . Diamond Izz and Marian have unconsciously used two of the phrases associated with Tess.

Revision questions on Phase the Sixth

1 How far do you find Alec's conversion convincing? You should refer closely to the text in your answer.

2 Write an essay on the use of letters in this section.

3 Indicate the reasons for Tess being under gathering pressure to accept Alec's offers.

4 Write an account of the threshing of the last wheat-rick at Flintcomb-Ash farm.

5 Write an account of events which led to the Durbeyfields having to move.

6 In what ways does Hardy show his sense of the novel's overall structure in this section?

Phase the Seventh Chapter 53

The Clares await the arrival of Angel. He is badly broken in health, almost collapses on arrival, and reads Tess's last poignant letter denouncing him for his cruelty to her. The next morning he sends a note to Marlott, and in a few days gets a reply from Joan which tells him that she cannot say where Tess is 'temperly biding'. He re-reads Tess's earlier letter, and that written by Izz and Marian, and then decides to go in search of Tess.

Commentary

The dramatic change in Clare physically is movingly conveyed through its effect on his parents, particularly on Mrs Clare. There is also the fact that Tess's final letter has been held for his arrival, Clare's acknowledgement of its justice, and the letter from Joan which, like hers to Tess, would be comic if it were not for what is implied. His faith in her abiding love is shown in his recurrence to the earlier letter.

Crivelli's dead *Christus* Crivelli (c.1433–c.1494) painted some pictures which had the dead Christ as the subject, one of which is in the National Gallery.

temperly Temporarily.
'which alters when it alteration finds' This is from Shakespeare's
   Sonnet 116, the relevant addition being 'Love is not love/Which alters
   . . .'
Faustina . . . Cornelia . . . Lucretia . . . Phryne The first is the wife of a
   Roman Emperor famous for her loose living, Lucretia was the
   virtuous woman who committed suicide after being raped by Sextus
   Tarquinius, Cornelia was the wife of Pompey renowned for her
   virtues, and Phryne was a Greek prostitute who gave her favours to
   the rich.
he had thought of the woman taken and set in the midst . . . See John
   8,2,11.
the wife of Uriah being made a queen See 2 Samuel 11, 2–27. The wife
   was Bathsheba.

Chapter 54

Angel goes to Flintcomb-Ash, learns that Tess has returned to
the home of her parents, and sets out for Marlott. When he gets
to Tess's house he finds that John Durbeyfield has died, sees the
stone in the churchyard, pays the mason for it, and sets off to
where the Durbeyfields are living. Joan is evasive with him, but
eventually he obtains from her the information that Tess is
living at Sandbourne.

Commentary

The pace of the narrative quickens, and here there are a succession of journeys culminating in some anti-climax but with considerable expectation, since the reader is suspicious but does not
know the actuality of Tess's whereabouts. Note the description
of nature and the registering of change wherever Clare goes.

a tale told by an idiot See *Macbeth*, V, Scene 5, 26–7. Of life Macbeth
   observes 'It is a tale/Told by an idiot, full of sound and fury/Signifying
   nothing.'
HOW ARE THE MIGHTY FALLEN The phrase re-echoes in the text
   since it is with the 'fallen' D'Urbervilles that we are dealing.

Chapter 55

Angel puts up for the night in Sandbourne, and early the next
morning he sets out to search for Tess. He finds her in a

boarding-house. She is beautifully dressed, and tells him that he has come too late. She tells him that she waited and waited, that 'he' won her back to him, but that she hates 'him' (obviously Alec) for telling her the lie that Clare would not return. He finds that Tess has gone, and goes out into the street.

Commentary

Clare is bewildered by the thought of Tess – 'a cottage-girl, his young wife' – being in fashionable Sandbourne. The speed of the narrative is fast and sure, with Tess's appearance and Clare's contrasting appearance and reactions at the centre of the exchange. Tess is 'like a fugitive in a dream', and the scene is deeply poignant and moving for the reader because of its sheer hopelessness.

the prophet's gourd See Jonah 4, 5–10.
gazebos Summerhouses or garden pavilions so sited as to command a view.
her well-remembered cable of dark-brown hair Again the anticipation of the rope in the phrase.
It is too late Remember the original title of the novel – 'Too Late, Beloved' – which is recalled here.
the body . . . allowing it to drift, like a corpse upon the current Note the use of death imagery as another signal before the murder.

Chapter 56

Tess goes back to her room and breaks down (the landlady overhears this), her long soliloquy sufficiently indicating the anguish she now feels at her husband's return. The landlady retreats when she fears that somone will come out, and later sees Tess emerge dressed for the street. She notices the mark in the ceiling, hears the dripping, and summons a man in who finds Alec D'Urberville dead in bed.

Commentary

Again we note the speed of the narrative, with Hardy employing the device of the eavesdropper in order to avoid direct narration of the killing. Nevertheless Mrs Brooks does see that Tess's clenched lips are bleeding in her anguish and that she has been profoundly moved by seeing that Angel is, as she thinks, dying. There is something melodramatic about the spread of the blood-stain, but the discovery of the body with the small wound is somehow reminiscent of the small hole in Prince – and then, as we remember, Tess considered herself to be a murderess.

some Ixionian wheel In Greek mythology Ixion, King of Thessaly, was condemned to be bound to a fiery wheel which revolved through Hell. This was his punishment for boasting of having seduced Hera, wife of Zeus, king of the Gods.

a gigantic ace of hearts A somewhat melodramatic symbol but, in effect, Tess has just played a terrible trump card.

Chapter 57

As there is no train for some time, Angel walks on, intending to take the train at the next station. He is conscious of someone running after him and discovers that it is Tess. She tells him that she has killed Alec, and he tells her that he will protect her. They wander about for the rest of the day, Clare getting some food for them at a roadside inn. They pass a deserted mansion, and later return to it, having decided to chance spending the night there.

Commentary

There is some irony in the message Clare gets that Cuthbert is to marry Mercy Chance, but he quickly crumples the paper, per-haps indicating that those lives do not concern him now that he has at last begun to live in reality. The fact that Tess's mind has become unhinged is shown in her naive belief that Angel will forgive her now that she has killed Alec, that it was the only way to get him back. At this stage he is amazed at her strength, and again the associations of the D'Urberville coach are invoked. A terrible irony accompanies Tess's continued adulation of him. She continues in all innocence, Clare being the more practical of the two, but with no idea of escape, though Clare does mention making for a port later. But this is a journey, rambling and incoherent, more in love than despair. The deserted mansion proves a haven though, as ever with Hardy, gems of imaginative description enhance its effect, the shuttered windows being 'like sightless eyeballs'.

when I struck him on the mouth with my glove Tess herself was obviously aware of her potentially murderous intent.
the trap he set for me Again, the animal/bird imagery is implicit.
her Antinous, her Apollo even Antinous was renowned for his physical beauty, and was a favourite of the Emperor Hadrian. Apollo was the Greek god of music and the arts and of the sun.
unforfending Free, innocent.
Atalanta's race Atalanta was the swift-footed Arcadian huntress who refused to marry until she was defeated in a race. Losing against her meant death.

Chapter 58

Tess tells Clare the story of his sleep-walking with her in his arms. They spend five days in the mansion, and a sixth, but on the seventh there is a brilliant sunrise, and the caretaker calls, being struck by the innocence of the sleeping pair and thus not disturbing them. They sense that they may have been sighted and set off northwards. That night they sleep at Stonehenge, Tess lying on an altar, and before she goes off to sleep she makes Clare promise to take care of her sister 'Liza-Lu by marrying her. She asks Clare if they will meet in the after life, but he does not answer. At dawn the police come for her, and she gives herself up.

Commentary

The might-have-been had she told Clare of his dream at once is given a considered stress, and Tess's not wanting to move shows her acceptance of their present happiness and her resignation about the future. Her fatalistic 'What must come will come' runs together with her deep-lying humanity – 'the sight of a bird in a cage used often to make me cry'. Note that their stay at the mansion is followed by yet another journey, the physical one to the place of sacrifice at Stonehenge, a deliberately chosen symbol by Hardy to accentuate our conception – and perhaps her own – of Tess as victim. Once arrived at Stonehenge Tess and Clare encounter the edifice and the winds; Hardy, intent on the maximum association of this fated end to their journey and what has gone before, describes the sound 'like the note of some gigantic one-stringed harp' (a reminiscence of Angel playing which commands Tess's awareness), while Tess flinging herself on the oblong slab is expressive of her death-wish but at the same time a reminder of Angel's placing her in the coffin. It is typical of the generosity of Tess's feelings that she should think of 'Liza-Lu, and typical too that she asks the question – about their meeting again – which Angel is unequal to answer. The arrival of the police is dramatic and humanitarian at the same time as Tess is allowed to finish her sleep.

trilithon Two upright stones supporting another lying crosswise.

lying on an altar Symbolic of Tess as victim, as sacrifice to conventional society, and also of her death-wish – as she says later, 'This happiness could not have lasted.'

I believe to the sun Ironic, since Tess is thought of as pagan and unconventional, whereas in fact she is conventional and very aware of guilt.

Like a greater than himself . . . The reference is to Christ, who did not answer his accusers (Mark, 14, 60–61.)

like that of a lesser creature than a woman Not an animal image, but suggestive of Tess's frailty and vulnerability.

Chapter 59

The execution of Tess takes place in the city of Wintoncester. As the clocks strike eight, Angel Clare and Liza-Lu, who have just come from the prison, turn to face it and see the black flag, which indicates that the hanging has taken place, hoisted on the octagonal tower. They join hands and go on.

Commentary

This is a superb set-piece, the perspective established with the two figures, and then the detailed description of the places and architecture which compose the city and which are the permanence compared with the ephemeral nature of life. Note that the sun is smiling 'pitilessly' (a wonderful reversal of mood, since the sun normally blesses), and that the faces of the two 'seemed to have shrunk to half their natural size'. The reference to the ancient hospice, to the pilgrim and the 'dole of bread and ale' is a direct commentary on the heroine of the novel, a pilgrim in life, innocent, and one who has received nothing. The final paragraph is fatalistic, establishing the link with Tess's ancestors who, like her, were fated to fall, but perhaps having some qualifying optimism in the fact that Liza-Lu and Clare are together in life.

Giotto's 'Two Apostles' The Florentine artist Giotto (1267–1337) is referred to by association because of the fact that his religious characters had drooping heads.

isometric i.e. having equal measurements.

hospice House of rest for travellers – the hospice of St Cross in Winchester.

Gothic The style of architecture covering the 13th to the 16th centuries.

the President of the Immortals, in Æschylean phrase The serial refers to 'Time, the Arch-satirist, had had his joke out with Tess.' This version, while referring to Æschylus (525–456 BC), is Hardy's own – despite his denial – version of Nemesis, the power controlling human life and destiny.

Hardy's Art in *Tess of the D'Urbervilles*
The characters

Tess

She was a fine and handsome girl — not handsomer than some others, possibly — but her mobile peony mouth and large innocent eyes added eloquence to colour and shape.

It has been said that Hardy was in love with his heroine, an admission he himself made when referring to the physical original of her. I say 'physical', since Tess is a full and complex individual drawn from imagination and from life. There is little doubt that the reason for the immediate and continued popularity of *Tess* stems from the character. Take the two key words in the quotation above, and you have the clue to Tess's appeal and her fate — 'handsome' and 'innocent'. She is convincing and arresting from our very first meeting with her, when she (the only girl wearing a red ribbon — and we have noticed the effect of this unobtrusive symbolism) feels a sense of shame at the conduct of the drunken 'Sir John' as she walks on the green. She is aware too of the three young men and of Angel Clare in particular, but there is no trace of coquettishness in her attitude. She is proud, both in relation to his not seeking her out as a dancing-partner, and also with regard to her father's inebriated behaviour. In a superb analysis of what she appears to be, Hardy emphasizes that she still has more of the child in her than the woman. It is one of the many ironies of the novel that Angel Clare, when he goes on, turns to look back at her having noted that 'She was so modest, so expressive.' She is, but he forgets her and, sadly, this impression he fleetingly had of her.

Though Tess thinks longingly of the stranger who has just gone, it is quite typical of her character as we come to know her that she immediately shows her sense of responsibility towards her family. She goes back to a familiar dreary scene but feels a sense of remorse that she has not been helping her mother. Tess stands out not only because of her beauty but because she alone of her improvident and irresponsible family seems to have a core of moral motivation and practicality. When she learns that her father has gone to Rolliver's to keep his strength up, she bursts out impetuously. This impetuosity is again a mark of her character, but she is also sensitive and dreamy and, because of her innocence, she is almost born to be a victim, for she is soon caught up in her mother's schemes, albeit unwillingly.

Tess's first assertion of responsibility ends in family tragedy and, so to speak, scars her subsequent career. Her action in getting her parents out of Rolliver's prefigures her rescuing them and helping them in later situations, but this first action shows how fated as victim she is. When her father cannot get up – he has, after all, drunk too much – Tess undertakes the delivery of the beehives. When Prince is spiked she blames herself for dozing off, and thinks of herself as a murderess. But already Fate in the form of her mother has been moving against her, for Mrs Durbeyfield had earlier suggested that one of Tess's dancing partners might have taken the goods for her. Always in these early chapters we are aware that Tess is not mistress of her own destiny, that she is prey to her mother's moral blackmail and the indolent disorganization of her family. Her dialogue with Abraham before the disaster reveals her tendency to accept what fate has in store (she tells him that they live on a blighted planet) but it doesn't diminish the anguish for her when it comes. She blames herself exclusively, and this is the early measure of her capacity for a kind of martyrdom. It is to this martyrdom that she conditions herself as the various phases of her life bring new tribulations.

After the death of Prince Tess still tries to resist her mother, having some kind of instinctual premonition about her newly-discovered 'relations'. She wants to try to get work, but this is not possible (apart from anything else, Tess is the victim of economic circumstances too, and Hardy never lets us forget it). To emphasize the pathos of her situation, Hardy tells us how popular she is among her contemporaries in the village, and also how she acts as mother to the young Durbeyfields. Her sense of responsibility runs throughout her short life, and we note that she makes provision for Liza-Lu by bequeathing her to Angel Clare, another direct manifestation of her concern for those closest to her. But in these early days one other trait stands out, and that is Tess's intelligence when compared with that of her mother and father. She has reached a high standard in the local school and, ironically, she has been educated in a moral way though with no real knowledge of men.

Her naiveté is seen when she first goes to Trantridge and notes the newness of everything, though 'I thought we were an old family'. Her answers to Alec's questions again reflect her innocence, but the taking of the strawberry signals the beginning of her subjection, despite her instinctive resistance to D'Urberville. Tess has a natural dignity, being proud of her simple family name, but when she returns home her intuitive fears about going to Trantridge re-assert themselves, and she tries very hard to get light work in the Marlott area. This superstitious, apprehensive aspect of Tess's nature is very important indeed, and is seen in its mature form throughout the courtship of Angel Clare when her past 'sin' obscures her present happiness. It is not sufficient to say that Tess has a morbid tendency; it is that she is so situated in life and has such a vivid conscience and consciousness that she knows that she is bound to suffer. In addition to her mother's persuasions towards Trantridge she also has to endure the chorus of the children, whose hopes have been raised that if she does go they will have a new horse and 'lots o' golden money'. Tess is never less than tender-hearted, subject to the generosity of her own emotions (witness her strangling of the pheasants later), and she succumbs. As Joan prepares her for the journey Tess, almost in an aside, says, 'Do what you like with me, mother.' Unknowingly, her tragedy has begun.

The drive to Trantridge shows Tess's modesty and her spirit. In a sense, just as D'Urberville has broken the mare so he tries to break Tess through the kiss. Although he is able to imprint 'the kiss of mastery' she has the courage to try to rub the spot he touched, and cunningly to let go of her hat when she knows that he is going to kiss her again. Tess is not devious but here, with little defence, she escapes and proudly walks on. This is her first journey in defiance, her later journeys being those of sorrow, hope and despair. All reflect that striking independence of spirit which she displays in adversity. Nevertheless, Tess shows that she lacks tact, for on the momentous evening of the Chaseborough trip she gives way to laughter at the spectacle of Car Darch and the treacle. The result is that when Car attempts to fight her Tess withdraws into her dignity, observing that she has 'let myself down as to come with such a whorage as this is'. This naturally provokes her antagonists, and only the timely – some would say cunningly-engineered – intervention of Alec D'Urberville saves her from physical assault.

With the proximity of Alec she virtually gives in to embraces until she realizes that he has treacherously taken them out of their way. But even then he gets back into her good graces by revealing that he has given her father a new cob. It is the way to win Tess's body, for her family, her own sense of guilt over Prince, weigh far more heavily with her than all else. Tess, ever vulnerable, is lost. There is every reason to think, as she goes back to Marlott four months later, that her pride has been injured. She is only too aware of the fact that she is merely a mistress, that the man who sought her kisses no longer wants them, but still her pride will not let her reveal that she is pregnant. She also feels very deeply that she will never love Alec although she has given herself to him. The result is a deep and tremulous sense of shame. When she returns home this once innocent child knows what she has done and takes home to herself, as she did with Prince, the guilt for it. One of the most evocative moments in a profoundly moving novel occurs when she says to her mother 'I was a child when I left this house four months ago. Why didn't you tell me there was danger in menfolk?'

The divisions in her nature are seen with the birth of the baby, with Tess alternating between ignoring its presence and kissing it passionately. Always Hardy's psychological presentation of Tess is consistent, for the child-mother is beset by love and guilt. Also she has been reared in the tradition of superstition and religion and adheres to both. Thus her anguish over the coming death of her child is balanced by a determined and selfless wish for it to be received into the bosom of God – her guilt would be compounded if she did not ensure this. The baptism scene, with the children around, has more simple spiritual Christianity than sermon or dogma, for Tess *is* love or, as Hardy puts it, 'The ecstasy of faith almost apotheosized her.' Even after this her courage is not lacking. She tackles the parson head on, asking for a Christian burial for the child and, when it is refused, seeking the reassurance that 'it will be just the same to him if you don't'. The parson demotes dogma in the cause of immediate humanity. Tess is, in Hardy's words, 'a pure woman'.

Tess's morbidity is shown in her reflections after this. She ponders on the date of her own death and on reactions to it, but gradually comes to feel that she may be able to 'be happy in some nook which had no memories'. Her pilgrimage (I choose the word deliberately) is initially blessed, although Crick's opening words to her mention the old D'Urberville family and make escape from the past difficult. Her fatal sexual attraction is now allied to her mystical ideas, her talk fascinating the listening Angel Clare. She is aware that he is watching her, for Tess is all sensitivity. Her own sadness is apparent – Hardy calls it 'the ache of modernism' – but so is her communion with nature. As she gets to know Angel she becomes increasingly aware of her lack of learning, but it is related to her fear of the past and the associations that she is fated. In her naively definite way she thinks that she would like to learn 'why' rather than learning 'that I am one of a long row only'. This view is strengthened when she comes to know of Clare's bias against old families. She has the good sense – and the intuitive honesty – to tell Clare to call her 'Tess' rather than indulge his fancies about Artemis and Demeter. Throughout she has a strong sense of her own identity; Clare, as she learns, has a stronger sense of her image.

Tess is somewhat undermined from time to time, particularly by Dairyman Crick's story of Jack Dollop, for she can see the immediate connections with her own case. She is unable to conceal her perturbation, but puts it down to the heat, though her morale is boosted when she hears her three companions talking about Angel's preference for herself. Even here her feelings are subject to sudden change when she hears Izz say that being a gentleman's son he will not marry any of them. She tries to interest Angel in the other girls – she has some capacity for self-sacrifice – but the carrying scene manifestly shows Angel's preference for her. In his own words, it is a case of 'Three Leahs to get one Rachel'. Her magnanimity gives way to the strongest feelings she has yet been aware of and she admits her love. With typical generosity of spirit she helps to ensure that there is no estrangement between herself and the three dairymaids, but again she is injured when they speak of the lady who has been chosen as Angel's future bride.

On one occasion Angel is overcome by his feelings and Tess, impetuous and impassioned, responds to his embrace although she has been taken by surprise. His confession moves her deeply, but emphasizes the divisions within her. She is 'stilled, almost alarmed, at what had occurred', but obviously somewhat bewildered by Angel's behaviour after that. When he returns from Emminster and presses her she tells him that she cannot be his wife, a decision which 'seemed to break Tess's very heart'. Humanly she turns to the excuses which are natural in their circumstances – that she is of a lower class, that she hadn't thought of marriage – but all the while she is beset by her guilt. This is confirmed by Angel's story of his father's dealings with Alec, whom she recognizes from the description. This strengthens her resolution and, inevitably, deepens her suffering. Her noble nature makes her tell Clare that despite her love for him it will be for his good if she does not marry him. Tess wants, at least one part of her wants, that the truth should be revealed, and in her helplessness she wishes that someone would tell Angel about her. This is pathetic but in keeping with her character. Against Clare's emotional and more particularly his rational appeal Tess is ill-equipped to hold out for long. As she drifts 'into acquiescence' her emotions become more deeply entangled. She experiences jealousy of a stronger nature than she felt for the dairymaids when she says to herself, 'I can't bear to let anybody have him but me!'

The Jack Dollop sequel further hits Tess. But she knows that she will break down as Clare woos her tenderly. Tess now undertakes a fateful journey with Clare to the station to deliver the milk. She willingly creeps closer to Angel in the rain (remember how she had resisted Alec on their journey) and in this intimacy they pass the old manor house of the D'Urbervilles. Moved by the association, Tess makes the first of her abortive attempts to tell Clare 'my history – you will not like me so well!' Her confession does not embrace everything, merely revealing that she is a D'Urberville, an acknowledgement which costs her something in view of Clare's reported prejudice against old families. That prejudice being shown to be superficial, Clare asks Tess to take the name. It is a mark of her pride, her sensitivity and her fear that she refuses; it also underlines the superstitious quality of her nature, for she fears that it will bring bad luck. Already overwrought, she at last succumbs and agrees to marry Clare. The immediate reaction is the terrible 'dry hard sobbing, so violent that it seemed to rend her'. This reflects the depths of the divisions of love and guilt within her. She releases these in an impassioned outburst of love for the man who has at this stage no comprehension of what she is suffering.

Tess is ecstatically happy at this period, but always with her own secret knowledge. When the girls find out that she is engaged to Angel, her secret guilt is again much with her, and she breaks down before them. She is also undermined by Joan Durbeyfield's injunction *not* to reveal her past to Angel. She wills herself to leave the dairy and to go somewhere else, but Clare forestalls her, suggesting marriage on New Year's Eve. The fact that the banns are not called again reinforces Tess's superstitious feeling that she will never be Mrs Angel Clare. Omens continue, and when they meet the man who recognizes her on Christmas Eve – Clare assaults him – Tess is upset, a feeling compounded on her wedding-day by the afternoon crowing of the cock. Yet Tess has already done her best to tell Angel everything, and we can't help but feel that she is fated when she writes all in the letter which goes under the carpet and is not seen by Angel.

But the ultimate moment of confession is at hand. The scene on the wedding evening, with Tess having just taken the diamonds, the poetic anticipation of their marriage consummation seen in their mingled hands as they wash them, is one of the most terribly moving in the novel, indeed in all Hardy's fiction. It emphasizes the quality of Tess, the lack of true enlightenment in her husband. Before that there is the D'Urberville coach legend and the two 'life-size portraits' of decadent D'Urberville ancestors with their likeness to Tess. But if these condition Tess there is worse to come before her confession; Izz is merely depressed, but Marian is found dead drunk and Retty has tried to commit suicide. It is against this foreground and background that Tess tells Angel of her 'sin'; what follows afterwards, in his inability to accept that she is what she has always been, fundamentally pure, changes the course of their lives. Tess married is Tess victim; for her there is no escaping her fate.

Tess's simple faith makes her believe that Angel, to her almost a god, will forgive her. She is quickly and searingly disillusioned. Abjectly, she says that she will do whatever Angel asks her to do. It is a sad but tacit recognition of the subordinate role of the woman in the relationship. There is the usual pathetic quality in

Tess when she follows Angel silently as he proceeds on his listless way. But such is her force of feeling tht she upbraids Angel in her despair, telling him that what he is feeling is in his own mind. His wooden responses move her towards suicide – we should note that the death-wish because of her guilt is an ever-present in Tess's consciousness – but his control over her turns her away from this. The contiguity without intimacy is daily death to Tess. Always she sacrifices herself, and even offers Angel divorce – unthinkable in the period – in an attempt to free him from the marriage. Her projected suicide with the cord from the box, which anticipates her later hanging, shows how Angel comes before all else, only the thought of scandal attaching to her name preventing her from carrying this out.

Tess is loyal beyond endurance. She feels that the longer they stay together, the more chance there is of Angel breaking down, giving in to his emotions against his judgement. But when she sees the way that his mind is working she determines to go home, thus giving him the freedom he wishes, and which is subconsciously expressed in his sleep-walking when he places her in the stone coffin. That incident, and Tess's protective watchfulness over him, is anguish for her, for she has to hear from his sleeping self what she cannot hear from his waking one – 'My poor, poor Tess – my dearest, darling Tess! So sweet, so good, so true!' Yes indeed, this is definitive of Tess, but she is fated not to be spoken to consciously in this way until the final sequence, when it is too late.

Tess is broken down by the 'severity of the decree' whereby Angel dictates the terms of their separation. Arrived back home, for the second time without a husband, Tess is upbraided by her mother for telling Angel the truth about herself. As if this was not enough, she is made more insecure by noting the fact that there is no place in the communal bedroom for her now, and when she overhears her mother tell 'Sir John' her news she is upset by her father casting doubts upon whether she is really married. When she leaves home again she is indeed alone, and now impoverished. The responsibility she has always shown to her family means that she has paid for her keep and seen to their needs. But her delicacy and pride refuse to let her make a direct approach to her husband's parents for help. At the height of her wretchedness, in one of her journeys in despair, Tess sleeps in a wood and, disturbed by noises during the night, wakes to find around her the dead and dying birds following a shooting party. Her reaction shows once again the rare quality she possesses. She strangles those who are dying (she is to be strangled herself legally much later) in order to put them out of their misery. She says 'I be not mangled, and I be not bleeding, and I have two hands to feed and clothe me.' Even in her extremity Tess has the humane perspective to consider others worse off than herself. She is in effect a victim among victims.

Tess as fieldwoman reaches her lowest economic ebb, but still her loyalty to Angel is unimpaired before Alec reappears on the scene. She deliberately minimizes her sexual appeal, wearing her oldest field-gown and cutting off her eyebrows. Reunited with Marian, she keeps to her unvoiced dignity of being Angel Clare's wife, and this too sustains her. There is one occasion when she faces in the direction where she imagines South America to be, and 'blew out a passionate kiss upon the snowy wind'. Shortly afterwards she learns about Angel's invitation to Izz, and doubts begin to assail her. Her pride is in abeyance, her own circumstances lowering, and at last she sinks her pride and visits Emminster to see the Clare parents. But Tess is humiliated by the brothers and by Mercy Chant, not verbally or directly, but merely because she sees that they are 'superior' and that they lack true Christian humility and charity. It says much for Tess's endurance, for her stamina, for her fortitude, that she never gives up despite this latest chapter of sorrow.

Tess's meeting with Alec D'Urberville is the beginning of their end. She is always sensitive to people and events, and in the convert she sees 'a grim incongruity', but although her attitude to Alec is one of passionate rejection, the omens dog her as they always have, the meeting by the Cross with its legend being supplemented as Tess sees Izz being courted by Amby Seedling. Tess, like Izz, is to make do with an inferior lover. Ever susceptible, she allows Alec to cross-question her about Angel, and although she defends her husband, she is forced to see the rational conclusion that anyone would draw about her absent husband while she is existing in these deprived conditions.

Tess continues her work under relentless pressures, both mechanical – the threshing-machine – and impassioned – Alec. Tess strikes him on the face with her glove, an anticipation of the later murder, but it is her words afterwards which are peculiarly significant. They reveal how she feels about herself, the sense of fate which characterizes her so strongly: 'Whip me, crush me; you need not mind those people under the rick! I shall not cry out. Once victim, always victim – that's the law!' But from this passionate response she is worn down by circumstances and the complete silence of Angel. She lets Alec walk with her, and he uses the proven bait of her family and what he can do for them to draw her to him. She is conscious of her weakness, ever-conscious of her responsibilities, and writes to Angel, confiding to him that she is 'so exposed to temptation'. This moving letter is the real Tess – generous, loyal, loving, faithful, forlorn without a cloying self-pity, self-denying, the genuine pathos of her situation moving her to identify herself with the nature she loves but which is now changed for her – 'The daylight has nothing to show me, since you are not here'.

She returns in the belief that her mother is dying, is still beset by Alec, and has to face the immediate problems after her father's death. Although she feels in these trials that she shouldn't have come home, we know Tess too well; she was fated to, and she was compelled by her own loyalties. She becomes bitter, at last realizing the extent of Angel's selfishness, and writing to him 'You are cruel, cruel indeed! I will try to forget you. It is all injustice I have received at your hands!' And gradually, perhaps inevitably, she feels that Alec 'in a physical sense' is her real husband. The journey to Kingsbere (to the family tomb and to moral death) with its attendant degradation, sees Tess herself wishing for death. Her tragedy is that she has to live on as the victim she knows she is. When Angel first sees her on his return he is looking at Alec D'Urberville's mistress. She has sacrificed herself in the interests of her family.

The final phase reflects the impetuosity of Tess in the murder, but before she stabs Alec we have to suffer her anguish as she upbraids him for telling her that Angel would not return. We should note at once that what moves her greatly is the thought that Angel, broken in health, is dying. It is typical of Tess that she should respond in this way, for others' needs are always greater than her own. It is also typical that she should confess immediately to Angel what she has done – there is no guile in Tess. For Tess, happiness is to be with Angel, and the days spent in the deserted house are for her the realization of her love. She has that individual, mystical sense which we noted earlier and which contributes to the complexity of her character. She tells Angel – and it is a measure of her insecurity – 'I do not wish to outlive your present feeling for me'. It is as if Tess has reached this peak, and knows that there can only be descent. Her essentially gentle nature has given way to something alien to her – the extreme of violence in her own extremity. Yet in a sense it has been a release, and the guilt that has followed her throughout her life does not obtrude upon her after her most violent deed. She has complete clarity of thought, knowing that her life can only last a matter of weeks. Her last thought is expressive of her selflessness when she urges Clare to take care of 'Liza-Lu who has 'all the best of me without the bad of me'. We cannot accept this self-denigration, which continues when she is taken by the police and says to Angel, 'I shall not live for you to despise me!' It is the sublime irony. Tess merits compassion. It is impossible to despise what is good.

The 'Pure Woman' has been 'Faithfully Presented'. The heroine who gives her name to the novel is a vibrant, tremulous, guilt-ridden and suffering woman. She has little happiness and is much abused, yet her own deep humanity is always in evidence, whether it is in simple responsibility to her family or in putting dying pheasants out of their misery. She is somewhat lacking in humour, but in the light of her circumstances and her experiences we cannot wonder at this. With Tess there is a running sense of what might-have-been. She might have been a teacher, but such is Hardy's control of her character, both without and within, that we feel as she feels, that she is fated to be what she is and to suffer as she does. If her own view is sombre, it is because she has moral sense and a scrupulous conscience, allied to an innocence which is unsullied by what she endures. There is no more complete portrait of a woman in English fiction and, it must be added, certainly no more convincing a woman from the English agricultural class. Tess exemplifies the woman who is submissive by compulsion (with Alec) but rejects in the first phase the immorality of living with him. She is submissive to her family, but rejects their indolence and casual opportunism. She is submissive to Angel, possessing a loyalty which is almost beyond endurance, and she rejects her heart by accepting the economic blackmail of Alec. Her honesty is almost terrifying in its directness, and her moral sense is not undermined by her experiences. Tess's crime of passion means that she will be hanged, but we are left with the overwhelming feeling that she has been wronged, that sensitivity and inherent goodness of character have been violated, that man has completed his inhumanity to woman.

Angel Clare

Though not cold-natured, he was rather bright than hot.

Some critics have seen Angel simplistically and unsympathetically yet, as with Tess, there is a degree of complexity in his presentation. Experience changes him, but too late, and he realizes that he has been in error and that life is not about theories but about living. His name has ironic associations, though Hardy in fact took it from a mural tablet in Stinsford Church. Angel, like his creator, is an agnostic, at variance with his father, who is an Anglican minister of strict belief and courageous practice. Unlike his brothers, who have followed the family's Anglican traditions in much the same way as they follow current tastes in dress, literature and art, Angel has decided to become a farmer. Though Tess looks longingly at him when she first sees him on the village green, he hardly notices her. He pursues his essentially rational way of life, examining the bases of philosophy, thought and religion, but his life experience is so limited that when he finds himself caught up in a situation with Tess he finds that his so-called enlightenment is unequal to the personal demands made on him. His confession to Tess is sordidly human; her confession to him is on a plane of suffering and violation which he cannot comprehend. Although he considers himself a man of independent outlook, he is really conditioned by the beliefs and practices of the age in which he has grown up. Much as he wishes to carve out his own life, he cannot overcome the influences which have made him what he is. Yet here there is some complexity in his presentation. Angel the man thinks to instruct Tess the woman, to improve her, to make her a fit intellectual helpmeet to him. There is a touch of condescension in this, yet he recognizes Tess's essentially spiritual nature. Angel the man goes home to his parents and confides to them that he is going to marry a girl from a different class. This takes moral courage and, much later, when Tess has told him about her 'sin', he passionately asserts to his parents her purity and innocence. And this is where the complexity lies. He knows that Tess is innocent in terms of *motive*, *practice* and *living*, but although his reason tells him this his emotions will not let him accept it. Hardy calls this his 'conventional standard of judgment'; Angel is a Victorian although he does not think of himself as such.

Angel is initially attracted to Tess because of her unusual spiritual qualities and, although not a highly-sexed man, he finds her irresistible in the lush sensual atmosphere of the dairy and the surroundings and the weather. The fact that Tess holds out for so long is a tribute to her strength of character and conscience. But Angel is obdurate, and from the moment that he kisses her and she kisses him back, he is relentless in his determination to make her his wife. When she confesses that she is descended from the D'Urberville line, he takes this to be the sum total of what she has to tell him. If Tess is fated, so is Angel – fated that the letter of confession which would probably have prevented his marriage is put under the carpet, so that he never sees it. Angel possesses a curious form of insensitivity, for he arranges for the honeymoon to be in the D'Urberville mansion where the portraits are recognizably if grotesquely like Tess, and he also tells her the legend of the D'Urberville coach. It is almost as if he has an inverted snobbery in his make-up. Having affected to despise old families he now takes some secret pride in his wife's being related to one.

Angel's confession to Tess leads her to say what she has wished to say for so long. His reaction is that of a man stabbed to the heart. He would be the last to admit it, but all that his enlightenment comes to is the tacit acceptance that there is one law for a man and another for a woman. He has been in love with the image of Tess – the ideal milkmaid, soft, pliant, relying on him, accepting his standards. Now he finds that she is, as he puts it, another woman. The fact that she has had the supreme honesty and trust to reveal what she could have concealed hardly registers with him, for such was his trust in the image he loved that her story overthrows his faith in humanity. He becomes ill with thinking, but although there are one or two occasions when he could have given in to Tess either from love or compassion, he does not do so. His feelings run deep. Just as he dreamed about assaulting the Trantridge man who had insulted Tess, so his obsessional thought now causes him to sleepwalk and to take Tess in his arms. The deep love he feels for her is ironically revealed, and the deep divisions that accompany that love too. He kisses her, but he also places her in the stone coffin; he is loving her and burying her away from sight, perhaps to conceal her shame, but more likely this is expressive of his wish to get rid of her, his wish that she had not come into his life if she is to prove false to his standards.

Yet there are other facets of Angel's character which show his sensitivity. He does not try to force Tess sexually, and this is not just because he is perhaps weakly sexed, but because he has a sense of honour and respects her. When he carries Tess over the flood he is reminded that 'he was somewhat unfairly taking advantage of an accidental position', and once when he takes her in his arms he checks the kiss that should have followed, asking Tess to forgive him for the liberty he has taken. The above two examples show that Clare is seen in contrast to Alec throughout; he is good, he is considerate, he is (before the revelation) kind, but always we wish that there was more flesh and blood, just a little more animalism about him. Yet there is little doubt that in depicting him Hardy is being true to his conception of fate; Tess has been seduced by a fake gentleman and now gets a moral and philosophical gentleman by way of contrast.

After Tess's disclosure, Angel continues to treat her courteously, but he is intent on himself and not on her. Although he cannot bear to see her demeaning herself, he is strong-willed enough – some would say selfish – to resist the temptation of being daily close to her. He has the practical common sense, however, to see that this cannot continue. In his way he makes generous provision for her, but in putting money into her hands he is in no way compensating for his lack of warmth. He, unlike D'Urberville, is able to subdue the flesh to the spirit.

So obdurate has Angel been, that it is not until he is away from Tess that he comes to appreciate her true quality. He tries to find excuses for what he has done, saying to himself, 'O Tess! If you had only told me sooner, I would have forgiven you.' We doubt the truth of this, but we see how deeply her revelation has eaten into him when he, in impetuous reaction, asks Izz Huett to go to Brazil with him as his mistress. This offer reveals his shaken faith, more, his shaken morality but, worst of all, it shows his capacity to hurt unthinkingly, since he withdraws the offer almost as a reflex when he learns from Izz that nobody could have loved him as Tess did. Angel underestimates Tess's pride, which prevented her for such a long time from seeking the help which would have been forthcoming. His embargo on her writing to him is also needlessly hurtful, since he was writing to his parents while he was away. Angel's judgement of Tess is both narrow and selfish. For all his analytical thinking, Angel has very sparse wisdom. Life exposes him. He is so little versed in the ways of the world that he does not stop to consider that he has left Tess exposed to temptations, that his desertion has nothing in it for her, though she contrives for so long to live on in blind worship.

After the words of a chance acquaintance in Brazil, Clare softens in his attitude towards Tess. His memory invests her with something of her living reality, and when he does return and reads at his parents' home that last abject letter which Tess wrote, the full force of what he has done comes home to him. It is, of course, too late but, despite his virtually broken health, he goes after her. On the way he pays for Durbeyfield's stone, and is more bewildered than shocked when he sees Tess at the boarding-house at Sandbourne. When she catches up with him, he is at first incredulous of her story that she has killed Alec, but when he does come to believe it we see what life experience has done for Angel Clare. Tess now has an indelible stain on her character, but Clare does not recoil from her. He has come through the fire of physical (and emotional) suffering into a new realization of what love and life are about. The result is that this broken man who could not take his wife in health because of his own limitations, takes her in sickness for the pure woman that she is.

But even in crisis Angel's rationality asserts itself. When Tess asks him if they will meet after they are dead we are told that 'He kissed her to avoid a reply at such a time'. Yet he accepts her wish that he should take care of Liza-Lu. Angel is of his time while striving desperately to reject its dogma. But the dogma of convention, if you like, rules him. Escape is only possible through suffering, the time needed for a true recognition of love and the real values of life. Tess's tragedy is in part the fact that Angel fails her in her time of greatest need. His heart is too easily ruled by his head, but in their final brief period together Angel comes to a true appreciation of Tess and the fullness of her nature.

Alec D'Urberville

Despite the touches of barbarism in his contours, there was a singular force in the gentleman's face and in his bold rolling eye.

Alec D'Urberville is something of a stage villain, and he is not helped by his language, his tendency to stroke his moustache and his constant recourse to that phallic symbol, his cigar. Before his dubious conversion he is obviously a man of loose morals, as we learn from his association with the Queen of Spades and the Queen of Diamonds, who resent Tess's rise in his favours. He soon decides that it is Tess whom he wants, and his forcing her to accept the strawberry is symbolic of his later forcing of her sexually. There is in fact little hypocrisy in his approach, but plenty in his method of getting Tess to Trantridge. The handwriting on the letter inviting her there to work for the blind Mrs D'Urberville is certainly masculine, but when he gets her there he bides his time, despite once hiding behind the bed-curtains to spy on her.

Alec's character is spelled out when he picks Tess up in the carriage to drive her to Trantridge. He is importunate, succeeds in giving her 'the kiss of mastery', and treats his horse as he treats Tess. He is determined to rule, to get what he wants, and to brook no opposition. He is an opportunist, and the Chaseborough Fair trip provides him with the right moment for seduction. Here he displays a certain cunning, for he meets Tess in the town, knows that she is waiting for the other work-folk, but follows them so that when the row breaks out between Car Darch and Tess he is on hand to sweep her up on to his horse. He knows, too, the way to her heart. Before he seduces – or rapes – her, he tells her that he has bought her father a new horse, knowing that Tess feels guilty over the death of the old one. Alec is used to buying his favours, but when Tess leaves Trantridge we feel that Alec is merely a shallow character who has satisfied his animal instincts.

But this is not the whole truth. After his altercation with parson Clare, Alec later comes to a reassessment of his sinful nature. His conversion is reputedly related to the death of his mother, but the whole incident smacks more of plot contrivance than of being genuinely felt from within. He puts up a feeble fight when he sees Tess again, and we feel that he is perhaps not shallow but a man of passionate feelings who desires above all to possess Tess physically. His following her to Flintcomb-Ash, his constant badgering of her and his contemptuous references to Clare show a man in the grip of an obsession. I do not think that we can dignify it with the name of love. Yet Alec has some redeeming features. He does provide for Tess's parents, and after her father's death he certainly relieves their position.

Despite all the staginess, there is something positive about Alec. In returning to Tess he shows that he is not merely licentious, though the brief insight we have of their life together before Tess kills him is damning enough. It is apparent that he demands of her that they keep up a small social position in the way of life to which they are consigned. D'Urberville is thoroughly selfish (though he does express a kind of angry humility when Tess insists on walking to Trantridge) but he is vibrant with life. He is a villain who does not pretend to be anything else. And some of what he says is true, as when he observes that Tess should not have been deserted by her husband and left in near poverty-stricken circumstances. He has none of Tess's spiritual imagination, craving only her body and reducing her mind to his commonplaces of social intercourse. He employs the only means he knows of to win Tess to him – the time-honoured method of moral blackmail and financial inducement, the latter not for her but for her improvident family.

John and Joan Durbeyfield

'He do want to get up his strength for his journey tomorrow'... To discover him at Rolliver's, to sit there for an hour or two at his side and dismiss all thought and care of the children during the interval, made her happy.

John Durbeyfield, the descendant of the D'Urberville family identified by Parson Tringham, shambles his way through life. He is incapable of taking responsibility, is shiftless, selfish, frequently drunk and, once he learns of his supposed status, beset by an overweening pride. He is happiest in his cups or when pronouncing, as then, on his distinguished family. Work is casual, often non-existent, and he does little or nothing about it. I think it would be true to say that perhaps he is the victim of economic circumstances as well, but there is little to commend him as an individual. 'Sir John' has been elevated in his own mind, and the result is that he will have conversation ready for his drinking companions. Thus when Tess returns home without Angel Clare, and Joan has to tell him what has happened, he feels it as a blow to his own pride. Durbeyfield has no sense of right or wrong in truth, and one of his inconsiderate actions is to forbid the parson to enter his house when Tess's baby is ill. He knows how much store Tess sets by the baby being baptized, but because of his own inverted pride he puts an embargo on the one crumb of comfort possible to her. Once a haggler, always a haggler; Sir John would sell his title, if he had one to sell, and at one stage tells Tess to offer it to Alec D'Urberville for 'a thousand pound', a sum which he reduces in a blabbing, rambling way to twenty pounds. So much for the honour of the family. He will sell his dead horse, until he finds out that the carcass is valueless, and then he rises to the occasion in an access of simulated pride and makes something of a family ritual of the burial. He is in fact all talk and little action for the most part. There are plenty of warnings that the fatty build-up around his heart will cause his death, but it comes as some surprise when he does die.

Joan Durbeyfield is seen first singing to the baby and embroiled in the weekly wash which began on Monday and has lasted the week. She is bowed down by domesticity, though it must be allowed that her spirits are quick to surface and that she displays a marked resilience to events. Her one treat is to go down to Rolliver's to fetch her husband back from his drinking (which they can't afford) and thus escape temporarily from the 'muck and muddle of rearing children'. At those times the children are left to their own devices, though one suspects that they are often watched over by Tess. Joan has the mind of 'a happy child'. She supports her husband by 'simple-souled vanity'. Although she has some misgivings about Tess's future, she has little positive thought for her daughter's virtue. The result is that she encourages Tess to go to Trantridge but, as her daughter later tells her, she gives her no warnings about the wiles of men. This lack of moral responsibility is summed up in Joan's own phrase 'If he don't marry her afore he will after.' On her daughter's return she initially upbraids her for her failure to get and keep her man, but such is her resilience that she soon recovers her spirits. She too, in a commonplace and even commonsense way, has a fatalistic view of life. As she observes, 'Well, we must make the best of it, I suppose. 'Tis nater, after all, and what do please God!' On one occasion she gives Tess positive advice, advice which in the context of Tess's guilt carries a particular irony. She tells her not to reveal her past to Angel, and shows thus that she has no conception of her daughter's character. Her conversation has cliché for its basis – 'What's done can't be undone' – but in the final instance she shows some spirit, since all the Durbeyfield worldly goods and possessions are, on Joan's instructions, unloaded and arranged outside the D'Urberville vault. There is little doubt that Alec D'Urberville's blandishments succeed because Tess is concerned for her mother, whose moral blackmail has contributed to place her in an intolerable position. Like her husband, Joan takes life as it comes, and makes the best of it. When Angel comes to see her to enquire for Tess she is at first distant but then tells him where she is; it is typical of her casual attitude, for she has a romantic vein in her that makes her think of her husband when he was young, and also from time to time makes her turn to her bible, the *Compleat Fortune-Teller*.

Mr Clare

Straightforward and simple-minded

Angel's father is a hard-working, earnest, zealous clergyman of the old Evangelical school. His ideas are fixed and narrow but nevertheless sincere, and he believes that Cambridge exists so that its students may take Holy Orders. If they don't their education is wasted. In a brilliant answer to his father, Angel counters the assertion that a University education is for the honour and glory of God and should be used in His service, by saying that he believes that it should be for the honour and glory of man. The most dramatic incident in which Mr Clare is involved is that with the then-dissipated Alec D'Urberville, and one must at once acknowledge his physical and moral courage. As he tells Angel, he has often suffered physical assault when he has reasoned with ordinary sinners. But Alec confirms the influence and effect that Mr Clare has had in his pastoral area when he says that he has been 'the humble means of saving more souls in this country than any other man you can name'. There is little doubt that Mr Clare, like his wife, would have liked Angel to marry Mercy Chant, but equally there is no doubt that had Tess made herself known to them after her long journey from Flintcomb-Ash they would have welcomed her, comforted her, and indeed made sure that Angel's wife would suffer no more physically. They are aloof largely, one feels, because of the haste of Angel's marriage and because he has described Tess in her role of dairymaid and child of the soil. But this does not imply set snobbery; rather it is that they are so concerned, so busy doing good that they cannot step outside their allotted tasks.

Mrs Clare is a much slighter character than her husband, taking her lead from him. It is somewhat ironic that when Clare returns from Brazil and his parents learn of the real reason for his separation from Tess 'their Christianity was such that ... the tenderness towards Tess which her blood, her simplicity, even her poverty, had not engendered, was instantly excited by her sin'. Their job is rescuing sinners, in living a good and frugal Christian life. They may be seen in contrast to the Durbeyfields, since they show great responsibility to their sons – both caricatures, too slight to be discussed here – and to their neighbours.

Dairyman Crick

Dairyman Dick
All the week:–
On Sundays Mister Richard Crick.

Hardy presents the dairyman and his helpers with a loving relish and with rare understanding, in the mellow atmosphere of an old-world farm. They are essentially practical people, and Hardy imbues them with a strong imprint of realism. Crick is a great one for anecdotes and for conversations which, unconsciously, influence Tess and heighten her reactions over her guilt. Twice he tells stories of Jack Dollop, the one reflecting on Tess, the other a kind of lighter nemesis of the kind she fears. He tells her that Mr Clare 'is one of the most rebellest rozzums you ever knowed – not a bit like the rest of his family; and if there's one thing that he do hate more than another 'tis the notion of what's called a' old family.' He has a rich store of local associations, on one occasion asks a childish riddle, but he is kind-hearted, and particularly so to Tess. He is present when the cock crows in the afternoon, and interprets it in his own way, probably thinking that the bride – Tess – is not a virgin; but he also threatens to twist the cock's neck, thus unconsciously pre-figuring Tess's coming execution. He represents work, con-scientiousness, some business sense; he is of the same class as those he employs, but worlds away from the Durbeyfields in terms of practical application. Mrs Crick has the sensitivity to note the unnatural brightness of Tess's eyes and the fact that she and Angel 'stood like waxen images and talked as if they were in a dream'. Husband and wife are somewhat canny, real people in a real working world.

The dairymaids

They were blooming young women, and, except one, rather older than herself.

Izz, Marian and Retty are strongly individualized, a tribute to Hardy's ability to draw living character without the full psycho-logical treatment which is accorded to his major protagonists. All are in love, or fancy themselves in love, with Angel Clare. When he is in the garden, they watch him; when they cannot get through the flood, Angel carries them, though the only one he wants to carry is Tess. They sigh for him, and at first are jealous of Tess. They reveal their own thoughts of him to her, and they indicate that he will not marry one of their kind, since he is a gentleman, and that in any case his parents have picked out a young lady for him. Hardy superbly paints a picture of the awakened sexuality of the girls in the bedchamber, as they talk to each other before they sleep. Sometimes what Tess hears upsets her, but there is no malice in any of them, and they prove to be good friends to Tess. Typical of their generosity of spirit is their reception of Tess's announcement that she is going to marry Angel Clare:

'We better than you?' said the girls in a low, slow whisper.
'You are!' she contradicted impetuously. And suddenly tearing away from their clinging arms she burst into a hysterical fit of tears. . .
They went up to her and clasped her round, but still her sobs tore her . . . They gently led her back to the side of her bed, where they kissed her warmly.   (Chapter 31)

When Tess and Angel depart for what should be their honeymoon Clare, at Tess's asking, kisses each of the girls goodbye. They are all moved, and Tess notes that 'The kiss had obviously done harm by awakening feelings they were trying to subdue.' They don't subdue them, and Tess has the terrible consciousness on her wedding eve of what has happened – Marian has been found dead drunk, Retty has tried to drown herself, and Izz is very depressed. This is not the end of their respective roles in Tess's life, for Izz tells Angel that Marian has given herself up to more drinking and that Retty is now hollow-cheeked and in a decline. Izz herself is something of a heroine, for when Angel asks her to go to Brazil with him she agrees to, but unwisely tells him that she couldn't love him more than Tess does – 'She would have laid down her life for 'ee. I could do no more.' She loses Clare, generously forgives him for his selfish proposal, but 'flung herself down on the bank in a fit of racking anguish.'

Marian is a great support to Tess at Flintcomb-Ash, and so is Izz when she joins them. The two girls sometimes change duties with Tess in order to relieve her aching monotony on the threshing-machine. More important they see her suffering on account of Angel and the relentless pursuit of her by Alec, and take it into their own sympathetic heads to write to Angel. This is after their meeting with Tess on the road during the Lady-day removals. It is a mark of genuine friendship and concern, almost as if these working-class girls feel the need to save one of their own. Though they are attended by pathos, there is a realism in their characterization which enhances Tess's, and makes her rarity all the more unusual and arresting. All are fated, but all are warm with the colours of life.

Other characters

Hardy is adept at realism in character by the most ephemeral of touches. Will we ever forget *Abraham's* dialogue with Tess about the nature of planets, or *'Liza-Lu*'s coming to Tess to tell her that her mother is ill? More particularly, 'Liza-Lu figures in the most moving sequence of the novel, made all the more effective because it is silent, with no dialogue to puncture the tragic mood as the black flag is raised on the prison to signal the hanging of Tess. Yet on another level Hardy uses stereotypes — like the other Clare brothers and Miss Mercy Chant, or Farmer Groby with his natural grudge against Tess for his humiliation. Sometimes the touch though ephemeral is effective, as with the parson whom Tess consults about the dead Sorrow. The man is out of his depth, because no dogma can answer to the individual sufferings of people like Tess who believe but question.

Structure and themes
Structure

Tess of the D'Urbervilles has a very definite structure, seen in Hardy's arranging of the novel into seven phases, each definitive of Tess's developing tragedy. These phases vary in length, with considerable emphasis in Phase the First on the innocent Tess, her family, the removal to Trantridge and the seduction. Phase the Second is much shorter, the passage of time registered by a sentence or so, but such is Hardy's sense of coherence and inter-relatedness that the length of the phase is made cunningly to approximate to the length of Sorrow's life, or the length of time it takes for seduction. Seen against the whole it is short and yet tragically significant. Phase the Third again marks the passage of time – here years instead of months – with its title 'The Rally' suggesting Tess's resilience, her determination to move away from that past life which makes her feel so guilty. It also underlines the rallying of her spirits and her emotions as she becomes aware of Angel Clare's love and her own love for him. But it is imbued with the irony that runs throughout the novel. The title suggests something temporary rather than permanent, and Tess lives always on the shifting sands of the present which move beneath her feet at mention or memory of the past. 'The Consequence' is of course ironic, for in this phase Tess passes through the various omens, tries to confess and at first is thwarted by fate, and finally does confess after having been warned by her mother not to do so.

'The Woman Pays' sounds one of the central themes of the novel. One of the reasons why the novel was unpalatable to certain Victorian reviewers and readers was the fact that Hardy is stating unequivocally that there is one moral law for women and one for men. The woman who transgresses sexually is the one who suffers – 'The Woman Pays' by having the baby, losing her reputation – and she also pays by having the conscious knowledge that *she* has sinned in the past. Tess is of her time and suffers because of it, but what Hardy probes is the injury done to 'a pure woman' by the unthinking male who violates her sexually and the insensitive male who lacks the character and moral will to forgive – completely and without question – the degrading past in order to make a loving present. The ironies of the title of Phase the Fifth resonate throughout the novel. Tess pays for being truthful, and later she pays with her life for killing the man who has been responsible for her suffering and who has denied her purity of motive and way of life.

'The Convert' continues to emphasize the deepening irony, for Alec is only a temporary convert and is tempted again by the sight of Tess. At the same time, because of his unflagging pursuit of her, Tess is 'converted' by him because of what he can offer her family. Alec the convert becomes Alec the born-again sinner; Tess the so-called sinner becomes the sinner in fact because of her 'pure' motives in wishing to alleviate the sufferings of her family. She is converted – perhaps subverted is better – against the husband who has failed to be converted by her love and her honesty. 'Fulfilment', Phase the Seventh, is also ironic. There is the fulfilment of killing Alec, the fulfilment of coming together with Angel (at least in the sexual and loving consummation he had denied Tess on their wedding night) and the terrible fulfilment of death, the final consummation for us all.

So much for the clearly defined structure. Within that structure there are interesting sequences which show Hardy's care for the detail as well as the whole. Take the marriage, which is significantly enough on the last day of the year, typifying the dividing of the old from the new. The broad structure of the novel has the seasonal background as an accompaniment to the inner seasons of the emotions, with innocence replaced by experience, illusion by discovery, happiness by unremitting tragedy. The human and the natural are closely associated throughout, and if there is similarity and contrast here then this is reflected in a like degree of association between the characters. The most obvious contrast is that between Angel and Alec as different types of men, the one essentially of the mind and the spirit, the other of the flesh.

The structure is affected of course by Hardy's – and by Tess's – fatalistic views. In *Tess of the D'Urbervilles* there are many coincidences – Tess seeing Alec as preacher, for example – where there is some doubt about whether they arise naturally, as in life, or whether they are imposed by the structure of the story as embodiments of the author's theses. However arbitrary some of these seem to the reader (like, for example, the convenient empty house which merely awaits Tess and Angel) they all contribute strongly to the sense of overpowering fate with which the novel is saturated. Within character itself in the novel there is a considered structural consistency. Early on we are prepared for John Durbeyfield's later death by Mrs Durbeyfield's report on his health to Tess – the doctor has told 'Sir John' 'You mid last ten years; you mid go off in ten months, or ten days' – and this makes his death, though unexpected in the context because it is *Mrs* Durbeyfield who is ill – natural. Similarly Tess's sudden tempers against Alec – including striking him across the face – prepare for the final temper which is murder.

The final chapter of the novel shows Hardy in complete control of the artistic structure. Not a word is spoken, no dialogue intervenes between the reader and the inhumane experience; experience of the legal taking of a life. The detail on the city of Wintoncester establishes the permanence of tradition and sets it against the impermanence of life. Only the flag registers the death of Tess, who in life has been so rich and vibrantly warm to us despite her ill-starred role. Each paragraph in its deliberate solemnity has the sonorous quality of the bell which strikes at eight, and that bell has the funereal associations of 'Seek not to know for whom the bell tolls; it tolls for thee.' The final statement of the novel is the natural conclusion to all the fatalistic events which have characterized the novel's action. In Hardy structure means the artistic completeness, the appropriate frame which encloses the tragic portrait: and that completeness is seen in the detail as well as in the whole.

Themes

There are two major themes in *Tess of the D'Urbervilles* and a number of subsidiary themes which feed into or reinforce the major ones. The theme of fate is pre-eminent: what will be will be, struggle though we may against it. The second main theme is the nature of convention, which condemns the fact but ignores the motive; thus Tess is pure in intention but a murderess in fact. The seducer escapes scot-free. The woman has the baby and suffers. Society condemns the woman but passes either no censure or inadequate censure on the man. Hardy faces this head on and in doing so challenges one of the central practices of Victorian hypocrisy.

'A pure woman' having once made a mistake, is helpless and cannot restore herself because of the conventions of society. Hardy cannot 'justify the ways of God to men', nor can he justify the ways of the Church. The President of the Immortals is inscrutable. Interestingly, while Hardy was writing *Tess* he was re-reading the Greek tragic dramatists, and their influence is apparent on the conception of the novel. That final comment that '"Justice" was done' is an ironic and despairing cry against the injustice which is being perpetrated. Hardy indicts the rigidity of society – and of course of the law – observing of Tess that she 'had been made to break an accepted social law, but no law known to the environment in which she fancied herself such an anomaly' (Chapter 13). He asserts that social convention is contrary to the laws of nature, hence the emphasis on the 'pure woman' in his sub-title. This innate purity in Tess is a fact, and it increases the reader's anger at the cruel irony of the double standard of sexual morality which was prevalent at the time. Hardy was way ahead of that time. Tess is not only the real victim of fate, she is a martyr to society. And other themes suggest that poverty breeds victims, that to have moral responsibility is to swim against a tide of indigence and decadence, that to tell the truth is to invite rejection. Against these there are the broader themes, like the economic and social changes envisaged in the coming of a more mechanized age which will reduce or obliterate the traditional occupations. This is connected to the major theme, since Tess as victim in the social and moral sense is by implication linked to the workers who will be victims of a new age. It is these emphases which make Hardy's novels 'pessimistic'; his themes are sombre, but they have a truth to the life of his time and, it must be acknowledged, for all time.

Style

Hardy's style is generally straightforward, though it must be admitted that it is occasionally ornamented with learning, and sometimes this learning is of an obscure or little known nature. There are references to Swinburne, one of Hardy's favourite poets, to Shakespeare (the epigraph to the novel is from *The Two Gentlemen of Verona*), and the text is liberally spiced with references to or quotations from the Bible, both the New and the Old Testament. The result is that we are aware of the author's wide reading and, by implication, a wide experience of life which has something of wisdom and authority in it. There is no bombast or straining after effect in Hardy. In fact, it can be demonstrated that the seduction of Tess and her hanging are treated with a rare reticence, and are all the more effective for it. For the most part Hardy's is a dignified and certainly disciplined style, admirably clear, smooth and continuous.

This straightforward style is sometimes strongly rhythmic, giving it a poetical quality – and remember that Hardy is an important poet, a poet of nature, which is assuredly evident from *Tess of the D'Urbervilles*. Allied to this poetic sense is an exquisite sense of balance. Take the opening sentence of a paragraph towards the end of Chapter 5:

In the ill-judged execution of the well-judged plan of things the call seldom produces the comer, the man to love rarely coincides with the hour for loving.

This is antithetical, the play on 'ill-judged' and 'well-judged' and 'love' and 'loving' providing an essentially rational appraisal, the weighing of things in philosophical perspective. This contrasts with the opening of the novel, which is direct, simple scene-setting of man against the background of his environment.

Hardy knows when to describe and when not to describe. Thus Alec is given a physical description which matches the superficiality of his character but Tess, although given a physical fullness, is given depth and a soul and spirit by oblique characteristics. She is ethereal, while in Chapter 20 she is 'a visionary essence of a woman'; this is directly consonant with her physicality when Angel sees her (Chapter 27), for although he sees 'the red interior of her mouth as if it had been a snake's' Hardy's account tells how 'The brim-fulness of her nature breathed from her. It was a moment when a woman's soul is more incarnate than at any other times.

For most characters Hardy needs merely a few deft strokes to emphasize distinctive traits, as in Izz Huett's being 'the pale girl with dark damp hair and keenly cut lips' or in the description of Angel's father as 'somewhat gaunt, in years about sixty-five, his pale face lined with thought and purpose.' What is quite outstanding is his use of the arresting image to convey the atmosphere of heat or of cold. Tess in Chapter 27 is 'as warm as a sunned cat', while at Flintcomb-Ash the rain sticks into Marian and Tess 'like glass splinters' until they are sodden. Metaphors and similes of a vivid and frequently of a visual quality are always to hand, and Hardy also employs personification effectively to convey Angel Clare's mood in the dairy after he has taken Tess by surprise and kissed her – 'The aged and lichened brick gables breathed forth 'Stay!'. The windows smiled, the door coaxed and beckoned, the creeper blushed confederacy.'

Hardy also uses the colour red as a symbol which has an anticipatory intensity throughout the novel, always looking forward to the shedding of blood (the murder) and the execution of Tess. There is also much white associated with Tess, obviously symbolic of her purity, and the interested student will find sequences which reflect the situation, for example, the comparisons of Tess to a bird, the use of the word 'nest' to convey spurious comfort or seduction. Particularly effective is the description of the cock which gives the afternoon crow, where the symbolism is cleverly combined in the colour – 'The white one with the rose comb' – while Dairyman Crick contributes his own mite of symbolism by saying to the cock 'Just you be off, sir, or I'll twist your neck!' It is the slightest hint of the hanging, but there are others, and the cumulative effect is to show us Hardy structuring his novel at depth and employing a pattern of stylistic devices to convey his tragedy emotionally and artistically.

Hardy's figurative usages are embedded in rich sequences of description and also in the dialogue and dialect of his characters. Hardy's spoken words, the conversations of his characters, sound and are close to the true speech of the time. Joan praises the baby's 'diment eyes' and 'Cubit's thighs!', the first a natural mispronunciation, the second a half-grasped association. In Chapter 3 there is a rash of dialect, with Joan telling Tess that she will be 'fess' (proud), Tess saying that her father has made a 'mommet' (fool) of himself, and Joan using words like 'larry' (commotion), 'plim' (swell) and 'vlee' (the one-horse carriage which could be hired). Throughout the dialect usage is completely natural and in character, though Tess herself uses dialect sparingly and speaks in two registers, that of the family and the more correct one which is a mark of her education. If the dialect is natural, then the dialogue, whether in dialect or not, is natural too. Alec has the tone and conversation of the man who is used to being obeyed. From Marian to Angel, from Dairyman Crick to 'Sir John', the spoken word in Hardy rings true. He writes fine dramatic dialogue which conveys the directness of the personality who is speaking. And even when, in moments of crisis, Tess speaks to herself, we notice that her consciousness is being released in words.

The spoken word is of course the major way of showing character in action and interaction, but the written words bulk large in *Tess* in the form of letters. In each instance they carry the terrible irony which is omnipresent in the novel. Thus a letter supposedly from Alec's blind mother inviting Tess is obviously written by Alec, the irony here being that this sets Tess on the path to seduction. What promises so well turns out to be ultimately disastrous. There is Joan's letter to Tess urging her not to reveal her secret to Angel. Tess does, and the tragedy ensues. There are Tess's moving and loving letters to Angel. Perhaps here the most poignant is the one sent on to Brazil with its broken phrases indicating a breaking heart – 'I must cry to you in my trouble – I have no one else ... I think I must die if you do not come soon ... Come to me, come to me, and save me from what threatens me.' Angel sets great store by this letter when he arrives at Emminster trying to forget Tess's terrible last note in which she says 'You are cruel, cruel indeed! I will try to forget you. It is all injustice I have received at your hands.' This in its searing appeal complements the note from Izz and Marian which told Angel 'Look to your Wife if you do love her as much as she do love you. For she is sore put to by an Enemy in the shape of a Friend.'

It is a commonplace of 19th-century fiction to observe that the teller is part of his tale, that the omniscient voice of the author is heard in the narrative in propagandist, sympathetic, confiding or rhetorical tones. Hardy is no exception. He will speak casually of Tess as 'our heroine', and although it may be argued that the illusion of reality is suspended, it is nevertheless an important part of *Tess of the D'Urbervilles* since Hardy is obviously putting forward a view of life. Hardy's philosophical or moral pronouncements are sometimes heavy-handed. They contrast strangely with the direct and often finely atmospheric descriptions which accompany states of mind or emotions in characters.

His descriptions ring true from his first-hand observation of nature, the imaginative selection of detail, intensely visual, being, as we have noted before, often poetic. Time is frequently recorded in terms of the country scene, as in Chapter 30 where we read that 'The lane they followed was so solitary that the hazel nuts had remained on the boughs till they slipped from their shells, and the blackberries hung in heavy clusters.' Hardy's descriptions appeal not only to the sense of sight but also to the senses of sound, taste, smell and touch. Mrs Crick always moves out the breakfast-table, with 'the same horrible scrape accompanying its return journey when the table had been cleared'. Note also the creaking of floorboards, the sound of harp and fiddle, the taste of garlic, the smell of fusty peat and hay. As Tess falls asleep the voice of one of the girls comes to her 'along with the smell of cheeses in the adjoining cheese-loft, and the measured dripping of the whey from the wrings downstairs.' (Chapter 17).

Hardy shows great sensitiveness to light-and-shade effects, referring to 'the gray half-tones of daybreak' and 'the stars ... amid the black hollows above'. One of the finest descriptions is the coming of dawn on Stonehenge when Clare 'could see between the pillars a level streak of light. The uniform concavity of black cloud was lifting bodily like the lid of a pot, letting in at the earth's edge the coming day, against which the towering monoliths and trilithons began to be blackly defined' (Chapter 58).

We have already referred to the omens and portents which are part of the imaginative structure of *Tess*. These are all part of the *irony* which pervades the book. The irony is seen in detail –

as when Tess pricks her chin with the thorn, an indication in miniature of her coming seduction and death – to the use of D'Urberville associations which form a running irony throughout. For example, consider the legend of the D'Urberville coach and Tess's unconscious recognition of the coach they go in after the wedding, a kind of *déja-vu* sequence. The coach is referred to again later, and Tess learns of the murder committed by one of the family, an ironic anticipation of the murder she is to commit. The family portraits at the honeymoon farmhouse are of Tess's ancestors and her features are 'unquestionably traceable' in theirs, which are marked by treachery and ferocity. Here the irony is in reverse, for Tess is gentle until driven to ferocity and murder by the 'treachery' of her position. Other ironic D'Urberville associations are in the first chapter when Parson Tringham tells Durbeyfield of his ancestry, and thus sets in motion the whole train of tragic events, and the settling of the family with only their possessions by the D'Urberville vault, with Tess uttering the terrible exclamation 'Why am I on the wrong side of this door!' It is after that that Tess succumbs to the fake D'Urberville who has followed her from place to place, and who can provide for her family.

The main elements of Hardy's style have been dealt with in the foregoing paragraphs, but the interested student will note the incidence of learning and quotation which was referred to earlier; there are times when Hardy overdoes this, but I suggest that the widespread biblical references in a novel which has a strongly agnostic tone constitute the final irony of the conception. The various styles within the novel manifestly suit the subject, the racy dialect, the natural descriptions, the symbolic usage, the omniscient control, all these make *Tess of the D'Urbervilles* a richly satisfying experience.

General questions

1 In what ways does Phase the First prepare us for the later complications of the plot?

Note-form guidelines for an answer:

(a) the Phase heading (b) the revelation of the Durbeyfield ancestry (c) the decadent behaviour of 'Sir John' (d) the club-walking (Tess with a red ribbon in her hair) (e) Tess as child still (innocence) (f) chance sighting of Angel Clare (g) the latter's lack of real interest but perhaps a hint that he will step outside his class.

(h) the Durbeyfield interior – poverty – Tess and helping her family (i) the high-flown view of Joan which leads to Tess going to Trantridge (j) 'Sir John's' drinking which leads to Tess's journey with the hives (k) the blighted planet and fate (l) Tess thinks herself a murderess after the death of Prince (his death the demonstration of the victim/fate theme (m) Tess's journey to Trantridge (compare with later journeys) (n) meeting with Alec (he forces her to take strawberry – symbolic of later rape) (o) Tess's guilt – 'I killed him' (of Prince) (p) Joan's persuasiveness for Tess to return (leads to seduction).

(q) Alec and temper with horse and Tess (later temper leads to Tess killing him) (r) the kiss of mastery (she later becomes his mistress) (s) Alec spying on her at Trantridge (equivalent to his later following of her) (t) Chaseborough – Alec's rescue of Tess from Car Darch (his later 'rescue' of her from poverty and her family's poverty (u) reticence in narration of seduction (just as reticence re execution).

Concluding para will examine the anticipations in terms of image, symbol, descriptions, dialogue which occur in this opening Phase and which reach their fulfilment during the narrative or at the every end.

2 Give an account of the part played by coincidence or chance in *Tess of the D'Urbervilles*.

3 *Too Late, Beloved*. In what ways do you consider that this was a suitable title for the novel?

4 What areas of *Tess* do you find humorous? You should refer closely to the text in your answer.

5 Write an essay on Hardy's use of symbolism in *Tess of the D'Urbervilles*.

6 Show how Hardy creates a particular atmosphere in any two or three scenes from the novel.

7 What particular characteristics and incidents of *Tess of the D'Urbervilles* have led to its being called 'pessimistic'?

8 With close reference to the text, show Hardy's keen sensitivity to nature in her different moods.

9 Write an account of the journeys undertaken by Tess and their significance.

10 Indicate Hardy's attitude towards change in the country areas, basing your answer on selected incidents in *Tess of the D'Urbervilles*.

11 In what ways do you consider that Tess was responsible for the calamities which befell her?

12 'A silence which might be deemed treachery to him.' Is this your view of Tess's failure to tell Angel Clare about her past? Give reasons for your answer.

13 In what ways do you find that Alec D'Urberville is inconsistently presented? You should refer closely to the text in your answer.

14 Do you find Angel Clare an interesting and sympathetic character? Justify your view from the text.

15 What is the function in the story of the milkmaids? Write an account of them individually and as a group, showing how they contribute to the effect of the novel as a whole.

16 Write an essay on either (a) omens or (b) superstition or (c) fatalism in *Tess of the D'Urbervilles*.

17 Write an eassay on Hardy's use of figurative language in the novel.

18 Write an essay on Hardy's use of his own voice in the novel. In what ways does this influence your own response to it?

19 Write an essay on Hardy's culture (i.e. his knowledge of painting, literature, the bible) as it is shown in this novel. What effect does it have on our appreciation of *Tess of the D'Urbervilles*?

20 Write an essay on either Mr and Mrs Clare or Mr and Mrs Durbeyfield, indicating the parts that they play in the novel.

21 Write an essay on the *three* most dramatic incidents in *Tess of the D'Urbervilles*.

22 'The last chapter is unnecessary.' Discuss.

23 Describe in some detail the interior of (a) the Durbeyfield home and (b) the interior of the dairy.

24 In what ways is *Tess of the D'Urbervilles* a poetic novel? Refer to the text in your answer.

25 Write on any aspect of the novel not given in the questions above.

Further reading

Other novels by Thomas Hardy, and particularly:
The Return of the Native
The Mayor of Casterbridge
The Woodlanders
Jude the Obscure

Biography

Young Thomas Hardy, Robert Gittings (Penguin, 1978).
The Older Hardy, Robert Gittings (Penguin, 1980).

Poems

Chosen Poems of Thomas Hardy, ed. J. Gibson (Macmillan).

Criticism

The Great Web: The Form of Hardy's Major Fiction, Ian Gregor (Faber, 1974).
A Casebook: Hardy, The Tragic Novels, ed. R. P. Draper (Macmillan, 1975).